Indo-Russia Cooperation in South East Asia

Indo-Russia Cooperation in South East Asia

By

Dr Prachi Madhumita Mohanty

GYAN

ISBN: 978-81-212-6152-4

Published, 2022

Published by

Gyan Publishing House
5, Ansari Road
Daryaganj, New Delhi-110002
Phone: 011-47034999, 9811692060
www.gyanbooks.com
E-mail: books@gyanbooks.com

Printed at: Gyan Press, Delhi.

Contents

Foreword

Prachi Madhumita Mohanty's splendid work on 'Indo-Russia cooperation in South East Asia' seeks to break new ground in the perusal of International politics. Indo-USSR cooperation has no doubt, attracted sufficient attention of the scholars in the post Independence India. But the joint endeavor of a resurgent Russia emerging after the demise of Soviet Union and a globally integrated India carrying on trade in the context of South East Asia continued to be a virgin area. The present study highlights the working together of both the powers in South East Asia, notably relating to defense equipment and oil. In fact, India is viewed as the gateway of Russian trade, mainly in the export of defense material to South East Asian countries like Malaysia, Thailand and Vietnam. Likewise the beginning of business in India by Roseneft, the oil company of Russia, led to its extension to South East Asia.

The present study has well brought out how in spite of the cross cutting relations in the globalised world witnessed in the move of Russia coming close to China and India to US, Indo-Russia relationship both during cold war culminating in the Indo-Soviet treaty of peace, friendship and cooperation of 1971 and after the disintegration of USSR and end of cold war getting expression in the form of strategic partnership between India-Russia, has withstood the twists and turns, ups and downs in the realm of international politics. The book waiting to see the light of the day has the potential to help the policy planners in grappling with some of the thorny issues of international politics in general and India's relations with major powers of the contemporary time in particular.

Prof. Shyam Sundar Acharya

Preface

Indo-Russian friendly relations stand as solid as rock. It has withstood many ups and downs vicissitudes, twists and turns witnessed in the global scenario. During the initial years of cold war when India took the leadership of non-aligned movement, it did not hesitate to cultivate special relations with the then Soviet Union. It stood India in good stead when India got embroiled in Bangladesh war and emerged victorious. With the end of the cold war, the demise of USSR emergence of unipolar world, the ideological umbilical cord uniting Soviet Union and India was severed.

But again the relations revived with the appearance of resurgent- Russia. India during globalisation turned its attention to South East Asian countries with which it had trading relations in ancient times. Members of the organisation of ASEAN earned the distinguishing label of Asian tigers. The resurgent Russia and globally integrated India who were traditional partners started cooperating in their trading relations with countries like Vietnam, Indonesia, Malaysia, Myanmar etc. These developments characterises India as the gateway of Russian trade especially in its exports of defence material to some countries of South East Asia. This has motivated the author of the book to pursue the study.

India, Russia and China are the architects of the multipolar world and are benefitted by it. No doubt in the globalised world many cross-cutting relations develop among the nation states. Russia has come closer to China and India to US. But these developments do not detract Indo-Russian relationship and their mutuality of interests. In organisations like BRICS they condemn terrorism which has assumed menacing proportion, of late. Even the South East Asian countries unequivocally condemn spurt in terrorist activities across the globe. Inviting of the heads of states of SEA nations on the occasion of last republic day in India shows our growing relations with these countries. The saying that 'One old friend is better than two new ones' is vindicated in Indo-Russian ties. There is a consensus among the Russian elite in strengthening old ties with India. Both have to carry on the joint venture of trade in South East Asia and beyond to maintain the multipolar world.

Acknowledgement

At the very outset, I want to express my deep sense of gratitude to Prof. Ajay Patnaik, SIS, JNU for giving me his valuable opinion on the subject matter of the book. I express my profound sense of gratitude to Dr. Shyam Sundar Acharya, Professor of Political science for his constant encouragement. His invaluable suggestions in improving the quality of the book have helped me in substantial measure. Had it not been for him the work would have easily slipped into mediocrity marred by numerous errors and blemishes. I have no hesitation in expressing my feelings that he has enthusiastically guided my intellectual journey all through. I express my earnest gratitude to Dr Gitanjali Panda, Assistant Professor of Economics, FMU for her valued suggestions on economic issues. In fact she has been source of inspiration for me.

My thanks are due to the staff members of JNU central library, Institute for Defence Studies & Analyses, (IDSA) New Delhi, ORF, New Delhi, and Indira Gandhi Memorial Library of Hyderabad, Central University for providing sufficient reading material for pursuing this study. I owe a great deal of regards and gratitude to my BABA & MAA & my two brothers and Sister for their special encouragement and support all through. No words of gratitude are sufficient to appreciate the encouragement and help; which I have been receiving from time to time from my in-laws family. Without the support of my spouse Chandan, this book would not have seen the light of the day. I am thankful to my little son, Daivik, sparing me for some vital moments to concentrate on the serious academic exercise like this.

Chapter - 1

India-Russia Relations: A historical background

India and the Russia share centuries of friendship and bonding. This relationship has blossomed into an equal partnership. This relationship goes back to the early 20th century when India was under the British colonial yoke and the Russia under Czar Rule. The Indian freedom fighters were inspired by 1905 Russian Revolution. Mahatma Gandhi cultivated close connection with Russia and used to carry on lengthy correspondence with Leo Tolstoy. He was interested in the similarity in the prevailing conditions in Russia and India. V.I. Lenin the communist leader of Russia viewed with interest and sympathy the nascent Indian freedom struggle. Subsequently the Soviet leaders in the aftermath of 1917 Bolshevik Revolution encouraged India to become free and independent. Many an Indian freedom fighter, who received inspiration from the Bolshevik Revolution, established personal contacts with the Soviet leaders. On the occasion of the 10th anniversary of the Bolshevik Revolution in 1927 Nehru visited Soviet Union and was profoundly influenced by the Soviet experiment. He developed a conviction that India as a poor developing country should follow not the capitalist path but a development model that emphasized social justice, equality and human dignity. In the post independence period under the leadership of Nehru India adopted a "Soviet style economic system". Although India was politically democratic, it was economically Leninist. (Jain, 2003)

It is worth noting that even before India's independence; an official announcement was made on 13 April 1947 on the establishment of diplomatic relations between India and the Soviet Union. Nehru was emphatic that India must develop close and friendly relationship with the Soviet Union. (Das Kundu, 2016) The free India set its foot in bipolar International system with USA (United States of America) and former USSR (Union of Soviet Socialist Republic) dominating the global arena as two super powers. That period was marked by the ideological rivalry between the two super powers. India in spite of its appreciation of Soviet model wanted to follow non-alignment policy. It was rational for India to follow that policy in the international environment in which it emerged as a free nation. But it was Nehru's genius to make the rational real. India cultivated special relations with the then USSR within the overall framework of non-alignment. During that time politically Southeast Asia and India were on different sides with most of the Southeast Asian states being anti-communists while India sided with the then USSR. Association of South East Asian Nations (ASEAN) also hesitated to support India's proposed security arrangement in the region before, primarily because it was seen as the Soviet Union's move in asserting its influence over the region. The deepening of friendship and cooperation with Soviet Union had been a priority of India's Foreign Policy during the period. Indian administration used to characterise its relations with Russia as very privileged and strategic. In the process India distanced itself from USA. The cold war, like earlier world wars was a contest on deciding who would rule the world. (Acharya, Mohanty, 2012) But this scenario radically changed with the end of the cold war. The world scenario changed and world moved from bipolarity to unipolarity under the leading role of US. India's Foreign Policy made U-turn after the dissolution of the Soviet-Union and the end of the cold war. The dominant role of US only was retained in every sphere like military, economy, politics, culture etc. Economically emerging countries like China, India i.e. the great powers tried to develop further and Russia also began its quest of its earlier position in the newly unfolding system of international relations. Both nations Russia and India support the concept of a multi-polar world which is divergent to the assertion of a unipolar world. This multipolar world supports the co-existence of multiple powers and possibilities in the international system; a collective security that is inclusive; greater regionalism to foster common regional interest; negotiated settlements; the possibility of independent foreign policy; and that international decisions be made through bodies like the UN that should be strengthened, democratised and empowered. The unipolar concept in contrast asserts the domination of a single hegemonic superpower. In describing the world in these terms, states, including those formerly in the Non-Aligned Movement or G-77, built strategic asymmetric partnerships with the US to maintain a stable subordination under a perceived omnipotent US domination. These nations become subsidiary beneficiary of the superpower. It is from the vision of a unipolar world that ideas like 'clash of civilisations', 'with us or against us', 'single path of development', 'military and superpower hegemony', 'regional hegemony' and 'client states' arise. A foreign policy based on the unipolar idea is bound to lead to military alliances, hegemonic policies and creation of regional hegemony that promotes regional tensions. (Chenoy, 2010)

Indo-Russia Relations in Cold War Period

The theme of the thesis highlights how Indo-Russian cooperation in general in the context of South East Asia in particular is antithetical to the unipolar world order witnessed in the aftermath of dissolution of Soviet Union as composite state and conducive to multipolar world order. Cold war has been a vital characteristic of international relations in the post world war II period. It was an era of neither peace nor war, between Soviet Union two foremost western powers UK and USA. The term 'cold war' was for the first time used by Bernard Baruch, an American statesman, and immediately picked up by Prof. Lippmann to describe the situation that had risen between the Western powers and the Soviet Union fought together against the Axis aggression their relations, though cordial, were marked by an undercurrent of mutual distrust and jealousy. There was a geopolitical tension after World War II between powers in the Eastern Bloc (the Soviet Union and its allies) and powers in the Western Bloc (the United States, its NATO allies). World was divided into two blocs each under the care of the super actors—the USA and the erstwhile USSR. In order to strengthen their own positions in global politics both these blocs started organising their camps. The United States brought the democratic countries in one bloc—the American bloc, through several regional alliances likes NATO, SEATO. The Soviet Union organised the socialist states into Warsaw Pact. During the Cold War, India and the Soviet Union (USSR) enjoyed a strong strategic, military, economic and diplomatic relationship. Over nearly forty years, Soviet-Indian relations passed through three distinct periods, coinciding with the ascendance of three extraordinary pairs of leaders, each extraordinary for different reasons—Jawaharlal Nehru and Nikita Khrushchev, Indira Gandhi and Leonid Brezhnev, and Rajiv Gandhi and Mikhail Gorbachev. The rise and decline of a political dynasty in India paralleled the same trajectory in the Soviet Union. (Mastny, 2010) Non-alignment, as Nehru stressed repeatedly, was not neutrality. It really meant Independence of judgment. It implied deciding each issue on its merit. India would not line up behind either of the two power blocs-then armed to the teeth and endangering world peace-and thus mortgage its freedom to judge every issue on merit. India wanted good relations with both the Soviet Union and the United States. It did not want to keep all its eggs in one basket. However, India's first Prime Minister, Jawaharlal Nehru, had a romantic notion about the Soviet Union and a soft corner for Fabian Socialism. This, combined with Pakistan becoming a US partner, led to closer India-Soviet relations. Soviet assistance in economic and military areas to India reinforced India's belief that the Soviets Union was a steadfast ally. (Pande & Thoburn, 2016) India since its independence in 1947 has followed a policy of peace and non-alignment. The roots of non-alignment can be traced to the legacy of the freedom struggle. The father of the nation, Mahatma Gandhi, conceived of a big role for India in the post-Independence world. The first Prime Minister Nehru was one of the leaders of the Non-aligned movement. It is said that non-alignment sprang from his head as the Ganges from the locks of Shiva. India has always expressed its view in favour of truth and justice. It was after India got its Independence in 1947 that the Nation became competent to form its own independent foreign policy. A friendly partnership with India ensued in the 1950s which symbolised the most successful of the Soviet attempts to cultivate closer relations with Third World countries. India's policy of nonalignment throughout the Cold War was to keep away as far as possible from the power politics of groups, aligned against one another, which resulted in two world wars in the past, might again lead to disasters on an even vaster scale. India's anti-colonial activism in the United Nations took the following line "We are particularly interested in the emancipation of colonial and dependent countries and peoples and in the recognition in theory and practice of equal opportunities for all peoples." (Mansingh, 2016)

THE ERA OF NEHRU

In the immediate Post-independence period India used to be looked at with suspicion by Soviet Union. Soviet Union used to think that though India had become formally independent it was still tied to the apron-string of the west and was their camp follower. But the Korean War (1950-52) removed this misgiving. As Nehru tried frantically to bring the warring sides to negotiation, Soviet Union was convinced that though India was economically dependent on the west, it was desirous and also capable of pursuing an independent foreign policy. This laid the foundation of a better appreciation of India's role in world affairs by Soviet Union. (Acharya, 1992) However India's relations with the Soviet Union in those first five years after independence were ambivalent, guided by Nehru's decision, to remain non-aligned and take active part in the Commonwealth of Nations. US administration announced in February 1954 its decision to offer arms and supply sophisticated military hardware and economic aid to Pakistan, which alarmed India. This close association of Pakistan-US did not go down well with Soviet Union, which also utilised this opportunity to develop a closer relationship with India. Although Indo-Soviet cooperation had begun much earlier, Soviet defence and military cooperation with India began mainly when Sino-Soviet and Sino-Indian relations started failing. (Abhinavharlalka, 2013) India-USSR ties really embark on after the death of Stalin and when Nikita Khrushchev was at the helm of Soviet affairs. That Indian Prime Minister Jawaharlal Nehru visited the Soviet Union in June 1955 shows the important geopolitical concern. Khrushchev during his Indian visit announced that the Soviet Union supported Indian sovereignty over the disputed territory of the Kashmir region and over Portuguese coastal enclaves such as Goa. The Soviet Union's strong relations with India had a negative impact upon both Soviet relations with the PRC (People's Republic of China), and Indian relations with the PRC, in the Khrushchev period. In the border dispute between India and China, Soviet union remain neutral but subsequently Soviet Union gave India substantial economic and military support. This stance of Soviet Union was one point of contention in Sino-Soviet relations. China Over ran Indian defences and exposed its weakness in the north-east. Nehru turned in desperation to the United States for supplying it with aircraft and other materiel. Describing the situation as desperate, he requested the dispatch of a minimum of twelve squadrons of supersonic all-weather fighter aircraft and radar equipment to be counter the Chinese forces. (Hughes, 2016) Nehru had some extra moralistic posture in Foreign policy and about the non-alignment policy. The unwritten assumption that because of non-alignment, India was not likely to be attacked by any big power was knocked off. Nehru and the elite of India became shocked for quite some time. The weakness of security aspect of non-alignment became exposed when China invaded India and non-alignment came in for sharp criticism. USA and Britain, of course, responded to urgent military requirement of India. But at the same time they tried to pressurize India to have a settlement with Pakistan and concede half of the territory of Kashmir. Had Soviet Union at that time helped China, which it was likely to do as a member of communist fraternity, then perhaps Nehru would have come under still more pressure to renounce policy of non-alignment and go for alignment with the Western bloc. But at that time of the crisis; after initial ambivalence, Soviet Union promised help to India. After getting promise from USSR, Nehru could silence his critics that conflict with China did not mean conflict with all the communist powers and especially Soviet Union. (Acharya,1992) In 1962 the Soviet Union agreed to transfer technology to co-produce the Mikoyan-Gurevich MiG-21 jet fighter in India, which the Soviet Union had earlier denied to China. Here it can be said that the Indo-Russian relationship really began in 1962. Nehru also invited the Russians to set up the Indian Institute of Technology in Bombay. Throughout his tenure as prime minister, he was open to good ties with all foreign countries and was one of the founders of the Non Aligned Movement (NAM) along with Tito and Nasser and it is a pragmatic policy. It is the pragmatism what brought India closer to Soviet Union. Nehru died two years after the Indo-China war, and his memory is cherished in Russia. There is a Jawaharlal Nehru square with a bust of the leader in Moscow's Vernardsky Prospekt. This statue was sculpted by D.B. Ryabichev. Of course, Nehru's first name being a tongue twister for many Russians, the square is known as "Ja" square. Its location is near the Moscow State University's metro station. Both India and Russia have moved on from their experiments with socialism, but their ties are so deep rooted, well entrenched that ideology and political disposition are not of any consequence. It was in fact Jawaharlal Nehru's statesmanship and vision that laid the foundations for this friendship. (Kamalakaran, 2014)

Era of Indira Gandhi

The unforeseen death of Prime Minister Lal Bahadur Shastri cast uncertainty on the minds of the Soviet leaders about India's future approach towards the Tashkent Declaration. In a letter to Indian President Radhakrishnan Soviet President Podgorny and Premier Alexie A.Kosygin expressed hope that India would honour the Declaration. The Soviet apprehension was due to feelings of right-wing political parties in India that Shastri had gone back on his promise not to yield Haji Pir and Kargil, two strategic places of Kashmir for Pakistani infiltration. It was believed by many that the declaration was signed by India under Soviet pressure and Soviet Union should follow a neutral stand on Kashmir issue. Allying the Soviet apprehension, President Radhakrishnan in a speech delivered on 12 January 1966 admired Soviet Premier for his "leading, noble and heroic part" at Tashkent. The Indian Government was assured by the Soviet leaders in term that the Soviet policy towards India would never change. Subsequently, Nehru's daughter Indira Gandhi, who, unlike her father, was a genuine realist bent on reversing the so called lopsided relationship with Moscow was ushered into power. India's ability to do so, however, was crippled by her disputes with Pakistan and that the USSR wanted to proceed without harming the basic interests of India or openly throwing Pakistan into Western or Chinese hands. Simultaneously, the Soviet Union realised that it would be even worse if India was driven into the Western bloc. Indira Gandhi openly told Premier Alexei Kosygin: "Nothing should be done from which it could be inferred that the Soviet Union treated India at par with Pakistan." India sought a treaty of friendship. In August 1971, after India had prosecuted a successful war with Pakistan in 1965 and amid ongoing tensions with both Pakistan and China, it inked the Indo-Soviet Treaty of Peace, Friendship and Cooperation with the USSR. (Hughes, 2016) In December, India entered the conflict and ensured the victory of the secessionists and the establishment of the new state of Bangladesh. It symbolised the diplomatic and military victory of India and changed the power equation in the subcontinent forever. This was made possible because of 1971 developments. It was during 1971, Treaty was signed for a period of 20 years with an automatic extension of five years for each subsequent period. By the end of this term, Soviet Union was witnessing serious upheavals and was on the brink of collapse. The 1971 treaty laid a legal foundation for ties between USSR/Russia and India. It displayed the existing alignment of forces in the region and the world, and played a pivotal role by helping India to assert its regional and global position and consolidate its special relation with the USSR. After the disintegration of the Soviet Union, India and Russia have taken important steps in cementing this friendship further. Overall bonhomie between India and Russia continued. The treaty was a significant deviation from India's previous position of non-alignment in the Cold War and in the prologue to the Bangladesh war, it was an important development in a circumstances of increasing Sino-American ties and American pressure. The treaty was later adapted to the Indo-Bangladesh Treaty of Friendship and Cooperation in 1972. Despite the 1984 assassination by Sikh separatists of Prime Minister Indira Gandhi, India maintained a close relationship with the Soviet Union.

Era of Rajiv Gandhi

In November 1984, after the assassination of Indira Gandhi her 40-year old son, Rajiv Gandhi, assumed office as the Prime Minister of India. Barely six months later, following the death of Soviet leader Chernenko, had the 54-year old dynamic, Mikhail Gorbachev, taken hold over the reigns of the Soviet Union as General Secretary of Communist Party of the Soviet Union (CPSU) Central Committee. Since coming into power the new leaders have tried to maintain continuity in their relationship which is bound by the 1971 treaty of friendship and cooperation. In the late 1980's with the improvement of Sino-Soviet relations, containing China got less a priority, but close relations with India received importance as an example of Gorbachev's new Third World policy. Rajiv luck in relation to China turned out to be better. In 1983, the Delhi-Beijing dialogue, initiated by Indira gave the impression of making progress. The high priority of relations with the Soviet Union in Indian foreign policy, the new Indian prime minister, Rajiv Gandhi, said a visit to the Soviet Union on his first state visit abroad in May 1985 and inked two long-term economic agreements with the Soviet Union. The two major agreements on economic cooperation were signed: One relating to Soviet credit to the extent of 1 million roubles (about Rs 1,000 crores) to cover specific Indian projects in oil, coal, power, machine building and ferrous sectors; the other on original type of long-range framework for setting the directions of bilateral cooperation in economic, trade, science and technology. Both the countries reaffirmed their commitment to the New Delhi Declaration on the principle of Nuclear Weapon Free and Non-violent World, which was signed on November 27, 1986. In 1993, the experts, diplomats and scientists assumed that President Yeltsin was not to ignore such friends and allies as India. Yelstin made an official visit to India where they signed a new bilateral Treaty on friendship and Cooperation in 1993. (Abhinavharlalka, 2013) In the wake of Rajiv's assassination, Narasimha Rao assumed prime ministerial office at a difficult and complex time. The cold war, with its comforting certainties, had ended. The collapse of the Soviet Union had confronted India with a completely changed and challenging scenario. The power configuration of the world has radically changed after the eclipse of the Soviet Union. The United States emerged as the sole super power with tremendous military political and economic clout. In the polarised ambiance of the Cold War, the Soviet Union obviously gained from India's friendship. India gained too, in both intangible and tangible ways. Nehru's policy of nonalignment justified by the "non-exclusive" friendship of the Soviet Union based on peaceful coexistence and non-interference in internal affairs. (Mansingh, 2016)

End of Cold War and Demise of Soviet Union as Communist State

As the immediate consequence of the collapse of the Soviet Union, Russia went through a period of dramatic domestic political change and uncertainty in the foreign policy arena. The end of the Cold War has witnessed dramatic changes in international affairs. With the receding of the two mutually hostile power-blocs and moving towards the "unipolar system," with the USA as the only military power, the entire international environment has witnessed a new emerging pattern of co-operation-cum-competition among members of the world community.

Russian foreign policy was following the collapse of the Soviet Union in December 1991. In December of 1991, as the world watched in amazement, the Soviet Union disintegrated into fifteen separate countries. Its collapse was summoned by the west as a victory for freedom, a triumph of democracy over totalitarianism, and evidence of the superiority of capitalism over socialism. The United States was delighted as its formidable enemy was brought to its knees, thereby ending the Cold War which had loomed large over these two superpowers since the end of World War II. With the disintegration of the Soviet Union, Russia found it herculean task to keep up the economic position with India. The infrastructure that gave support to the trade, economic, scientific and technical cooperation was practically demolished. The entire world political scenario has led to a complete reformulation of political, economic and military alliances all over the globe. On December 26, 1991 the Soviet Union was dissolved. It came in the form of the declaration number 142-Í of the Soviet of the Republics of the Supreme Soviet of the Soviet Union. The declaration acknowledged the independence of the former Soviet republics and carved out the Commonwealth of Independent States (CIS), although five of the signatories endorsed it much later or did not do it at all. On the previous day, Soviet President Mikhail Gorbachev, the eighth leader of the Soviet Union, resigned, declared his office extinct, and handed over its powers – including control of the Soviet nuclear missile launching codes – to Russian President Boris Yeltsin.

Mikhail Gorbachev's Perestroika with rapid political reforms provided opportunities for development of genuine parliamentarism to a considerable extend in the former Soviet Union. "More democracy – more socialism", "all power to Soviets" became the hallmark of second stage of Gorbachev's perestroika revolution. Democratisation of CPSU and Soviet Society as a whole became the key-word during the second stage of perestorika. Gorbachev increasingly came under attack inside the CPSU for lack of success in his perestroika, and rightly apprehended that party leadership would dethrone him. Hence he made an attempt to build his power-base in other structures, particularly in the elected legislative system. The 19th party conference made clear separation of power between state and communist party organs; brought an end to party interference in the affairs of the state, and gave only political job to CPSU. Euphoria generated in the mid-1980s by perestroika was quickly replaced by growing disenchantment stemming from hollow slogans. Glasnost campaign too was launched by Gorbachev. He successfully managed to persuade the communist party to embark on perestroika and glasnost path, but when CPSU itself became the main target and worst victim of the glasnost campaign, part of the party leadership as well as rank and file showed rebellious mood against Kremlin boss. Sensing the rebellious mood inside the party, Gorbachev sought to build his new power-base in the elected parliament. After the failure of the so-called coup by the GKChp, led by all the top leaders of Soviet state and CPSU that included KGB chief Vladimir Kruchkov, Prime Minister Valentin Pavlov, Vice-President Yanayev (except Gorbachev), Yeltsin made a real counter coup with the help of

Congress of Peoples' Deputies (CPD) of Russian Federation. Soviet President Gorbachev dissolved the CPD and the Supreme Soviet of USSR, the first democratically elected parliament of Soviet Union, in the aftermath of the August coup attempt. Russian parliamentarism that witnessed an upsurge in the final years of perestroika saw its gradual decline following the so called coup in August, 1991. The Supreme Soviet of Russian Federation, rather its leadership, cannot escape its responsibility in the destruction of CPD of USSR and its Supreme Soviet. Russian parliament that was used by Yeltsin to destroy the federal parliament and federal center finally fell victim to the power-hungry. Russian President when it tried to object his disastrous policies and obstruct his path to unlimited authority.(Mohanty, 2010) The Soviet intelligentsia took stock of its ideology and history in war and peace and, after a complex power struggle and debate, concluded that the whole experience of Communism had been a tragic mistake, "seventy years on a path to nowhere." Communism was defeated, not so much by reasoned consideration of the case for the free market, as by a sudden and sharp disillusionment with the Soviet past. The occasion for the inventory was the advent of new leadership in the person of Mikhail Gorbachev. So glasnost was intimately connected to the struggle to consolidate the Gorbachev regime. (D'Agostino, 2017) Gorbachev's decision to loosen the Soviet yoke on the countries of Eastern Europe created an independent, democratic momentum that led to the collapse of the Berlin Wall in November 1989, and then the overthrow of Communist rule throughout Eastern Europe. The decision of Gorbachev to allow elections with a multi-party system and create a presidency for the Soviet Union initiated a slow process of democratisation that eventually destabilised Communist control and contributed to the demise of the Soviet Union. Following the May 1990 elections, Gorbachev faced conflicting internal political pressures: Boris Yeltsin and the pluralist movement pressed the demand for democratisation and rapid economic reforms while the hard-line Communist elite wanted to thwart Gorbachev's reform agenda. The unsuccessful August 1991 coup against Gorbachev sealed the fate of the Soviet Union. The opposition in country got demoralised and defunct in that aftermath of the failed August 'coup' and lied low for several months without opposing president Yeltsin in the transition period. The sixth Congress saw the re-emergence of opposition to Yeltsin in Russian Parliament. Cracks were observed in the ranks of "Democratic Russia" block that had put Yeltsin in the helm of affairs. Yeltsin was no more the hero. Basking in the victory over the failed coup, he got the extra-ordinary power to hold the post of Prime Minister, to appoint his ministers at his goodwill without consulting the Parliament a democratic norm established during the years of perestroika to rule the country through decrees. The second half of September, 1993 turned quite tense with President and Parliament trying to outmaneuver each other. Majority of the members wanted to have early parliament election at the same time. Apart from this, lots of things were not clear about the timing and way to conduct the Parliament election. Most important question was what kind of Parliament has to be elected. The CPD members were not ready for a super-Presidential form of Political System in the country. It was difficult to reach a compromise on these issues as the Parliament and President had diametrically different views on the functions and rights of the new Parliament. Parliament has been pushed to the bottom of the priority list of the new political structure, envisaged by Yeltsin's constitution. The principle of Proportional representation helped strengthening the nation-state system of Russia. The Liberal Democratic Party and the fair Russia party are satellites of the ruling establishment, created with the tacit support of Kremlin clearly to exploit the nationalist and leftist sentiments of the people and split the left vote bank. The most spectacular achievement of President Putin is that he succeeded in bringing political and economic stability to the country by bringing an end to the chaotic period heralded by Yelstin's regime. Russia achieved unprecedented economic resurgence and gained back its prestige as a global power under Putin's presidency. Yeltsins regime was subservient to the west and working as a junior partner of US to defend latter's national and strategic interests whereas Russia under Putin has started asserting itself as an independent global power, often challenging the west and fighting for a Multipolar world as opposed to US plan to build an Unipolar World Order under its hegemony. (Mohanty, 2010)

Leadership change and focus in India

With the Asian financial crisis in July 1997 the 1998 global recession was witnessed. This exacerbated Russia's continuing economic crisis. A political crisis came to a head in March when Yeltsin suddenly dismissed Prime Minister Viktor Chernomyrdin. The financial fall down produced a political crisis, as Yeltsin, with his domestic support evaporating, had to contend with an emboldened opposition in the parliament. Somehow Russia bounced back from the August 1998 financial crash with surprising speed. In August 1999, Yeltsin once again abruptly dismissed the government and named Vladimir Putin as his candidate to head the new government. The economic reason for the recovery is that world oil prices rapidly increased during 1999–2000. President Putin and Prime Minister Atal Bihari Vajpayee in New Delhi during October 2000 signed strategic partnership declaration for both the countries. Despite so many ups and downs in Russia, Putin's popularity, which stems from his reputation as a strong leader, stands in contrast to the unpopularity of his predecessor, hinges on consolidating of economic recovery. In 2005, the Russian government replaced the broad in-kind Soviet-era benefits, such as free transportation and subsidies for heating and other utilities for socially vulnerable groups by cash payments. The reform, known as monetisation, has been unpopular and caused a wave of demonstrations in various Russian cities, with thousands of retirees protesting against the loss of their benefits. This was the first time such wave of protests took place during the Putin administration. The reform hurt the popularity of the Russian government, but Putin personally was still popular, with a 77% approval rating. In trying to reassert Russia's great-power pretensions, Vladimir Putin advocated a "strategic partnership" with India as soon as he became president. On his first visit to Delhi in 2000, he echoed Brezhnev by invoking the "congruence of long-term national and geopolitical interests." (Cherian, 2000) Putin reassured India that Russia would not sell arms to Pakistan. Weapons sales to India went up, including advanced T-90 tanks, an aircraft carrier, and licensed production of SU-30 combat aircraft. (Bulavinov, 2002)

The first major political initiative, since the collapse of the Soviet Union, between India and Russia began with the Strategic Partnership signed between the two countries in 2000. President Vladimir Putin stated in an article written by him in the Hindu, "The Declaration on Strategic Partnership between India and Russia signed in October 2000 became a truly historic step". Former Prime Minister Manmohan Singh also agreed with his counterpart by stated in speech given during President Putin's 2012 visit to India, "President Putin is a valued friend of India and the original architect of the India-Russia strategic partnership". Both countries closely collaborate on matters of shared national interest these include at the UN, BRICS, G20 and SCO where India has observer status and has been asked by Russia to become a full member. Russia also strongly supports India receiving a permanent seat on the United Nations Security Council. In addition, Russia has vocally backed India joining the NSG and APEC. Moreover, it has also expressed interest in joining SAARC with observer status in which India is a founding member. Russia currently is one of only two countries in the world (the other being Japan) that has a mechanism for annual ministerial-level defence reviews with India. The Indo-Russian Inter-Governmental Commission (IRIGC) is one of the largest and most comprehensive governmental mechanisms that India has had with any country internationally. Almost every department from the Government of India attends it.

Resurgence of Russia

A combination of factors like strong leadership and firm handling of the transition to a free market economy, integration into the world economy, the growth in oil and gas production and increasing oil revenues due to rising prices led to the economic resurgence of Russia. The main objective of Russia's efforts is to raise the standard of living of its citizens and bring the country's position at par with other major powers. (Das Kundu, 2006) The global economic recession that again started in 2008 has made Russia's position look somewhat weaker. But Russia today is undeniably richer and more stable than it was at any point during the 1990s. Russia has also developed a much more assertive foreign policy over the past decade. Its resurgence, as might be expected, has been met with ambivalence from the United States and the European Union, particularly when viewed in light of concerns over Russia's creeping authoritarian tendencies. While elements of the Cold War undoubtedly continue to define Western-Russian interaction, the terms of Russian relations with both the US and the EU have shifted fundamentally in a number of important ways, and it is time to begin finding a new paradigm to define relations between these actors. The resurgence of the Russian economy has ramifications for India. Indian business houses have started realising that Russia is the market for future investment, with tremendous opportunities and potential.

Indo-Russia Relations after Its Resurgence

India and Russia the two friendly countries can surely continue to have good and warm relations based on their proximity of the past. India and Russia can definitely look for convergence of interests in the international field. However, seeking convergence with Russia cannot be at the cost of India's quest for newer strategic cooperative link with countries like USA, France, Israel, Vietnam, Japan and South Africa. More realistically, with the emerging international system, Russia is very much accommodative in seeking strategic convergence with India. India is aware of the many alternative strategic options open to her, other than Russia, which the emerging international security environment provides her.(Kapila, 2000) In a 2002 joint declaration, he and Vajpayee pledged that neither government would "take any action which will threaten the security of each other's country, including in the sphere of military-technical cooperation."(Bulavinov, 2002) The two countries had agreed to move from a "buyer-seller" relationship to collaborative research and development, joint production of weapons systems, and strategic cooperation in oil and natural gas exploration, but mutual trade nonetheless remained "abysmally low." When Putin came to India in 2007 as the Guest of honour for the sixtieth anniversary of India's independence, the former ambassador to Moscow Satinder K. Lambah eulogized Russia as an "anchor of certainty in a sea of strategic flux." (Mastny, 2010) The levada center, the only non-governmental pollster in Russia and labeled a foreign agent by Kremlin in 2016 is distinguished by the comprehensive Russian opinion polls it publishes. In the 2017 poll which was out this year, Russians identified Belarus as their country's top ally, followed by China, Kazaakhstan, Syria and India. (TOI, 2018)

The scope of the review of literature includes three categories:

(i) Indo-Russia/Soviet cooperation, (ii) Indo-ASEAN co-operation in the International arena and lastly (iii) Indo-Russian cooperation in South East Asia.

Review of Literature

Chenoy and Rajan kumar (2017)'s book ***Re-emerging Russia: Structures, Institutions and Processes*** assesses the continuities and changes with the Soviet past and the way the Russian regimes of the past two decades have reinvented and reshaped them. This book provides a multifaceted interpretation of contemporary Russia for general readers and specialists. It analyses the Soviet dissolution, revealing the combination of structural and agency factors. It traces the re-emergence of Russia from a unique perspective that is neither Western nor Eurasian, but specifically Indian, located in the global South. They have also focused on how the stabilization of the economy showed the political benefits to Putin in terms of his credibility and popularity in Russia. Russia wants to enhance and continue its strategic cooperation with China and India and develop bilateral as well as multilateral relations with theses powers included as in BRICS and SCO. Russia has given priority to its security interest. It has taken a position on international issues and has reemerged as a major player in international politics. There is a consensus behind Putin's foreign policy with many countries of the global south based on appreciation of Russian positions and support for the idea of a Multipolar world where Russia has a role to play.

S.P. Singh(1987) in his book '**Political dimensions of India-USSR relations**' made an attempt to analyze Political aspects of Indo-USSR relation and Soviet support towards India during critical time indicative of mutual trust. This work aims at an objective and a comprehensive treatment of the subject. It shows that irrespective of several concerted efforts made in certain quarters with a view to stamping out the shine and glitter of friendly ties between India and the USSR, these two countries have successfully withstood all such onslaughts due to the basic identity of their interests. A critical scrutiny of Indo-Soviet political contacts, this treatise testifies to the fact that despite the changes in the leadership of these two countries and their differing perceptions of some of the problems, India and the Soviet Union have not allowed anything to sour their time-tested relationship.

Sharma (1999) highlights India s relations with the USSR from the day of independence that is 15 August 1947 to the consummation of second liberation in the form of the emergence of Bangladesh as an independent state in December 1971. This happened to be the most crucial period in the contemporary history of India in that it coincided with the formative period in our foreign policy during which India had to face many a crisis in the process of management of which determined the course of our relationship with the major powers. All important issues have been treated in detail in the body of the essay with particular reference to those controversies that caused much ripples on the otherwise placid waters of Indian diplomacy. The section dealing with the Bangladesh crisis covers a wide range of international factors that helped India to achieve this signal success. After weathering years of financial upheaval, Russia has recovered to become one of the ten largest economic powers in the world. It is the third-largest trade partner of the European Union, the fourth-largest trade partner of the Euro zone, and an essential energy supplier to the EU. This impressive recovery has made Russia an economic and political actor that cannot be ignored. This book describes the country's evolving policy framework and macroeconomic performance, from the difficult days of transition recession and the 1998 financial crisis to the sustained and robust growth since 1999 that is only partially related to the energy price cycle. It examines the improved Russian macro- and microeconomic policy frameworks— in particular the components that impact the country's fiscal and monetary systems, foreign direct investment, competitiveness, energy sector, social development, and state reform. The study also looks at some of Russia's remaining reform priorities and provides policy recommendations.

'Indo-Soviet Relations: the Rajiv Era' by **Bushra Gohar** is focused on relations between India and Russia which are deep rooted and very crucial. This paper analyses about the importance of both the partners in their foreign policy determination especially during Rajiv Gandhi's leadership. A country's foreign policy usually does not depend on the whims of individual but geopolitical realities, security environment and a lot of other historical, social, and economic factors, portraying that national interest is necessary component in foreign policy making. The two countries could work together to maintain peace and stability and go for better world. Soviet assistance was not limited to the supply of weapons and hardware alone but also to the building up of India's defence production capability.

Another important article of **Anuradha M. Chenoy** entitled '**India Russia Forging Ahead in Changing Times'** has focused on Indo-Russia relations and their attempt at constructing multi-polar world as the continued agenda. Here the author has analyzed about the major challenges for both Russia and India in a fast changing globalised world. Both countries have developed multiple geostrategic interests and have widened their interactions. Russia is closely associated with China, just as India is with the US, but both consider that in a globalised world, the old dependencies are over, and new inter-dependency is possible, where each country can have cross cutting relations without harming the core interests of the other. The Russian relations with China and Indian relations with US will not harm India-Russia relations, but have the ability to mediate between relations. Russia India relations have been key to building BRICS. Both countries understand this and are addressing bilateral and other issues as holistically as possible. Of course challenges will remain. In these circumstances, India has to rebuild on its strengths and common concerns with the Russians. They have to revitalize their earlier agreement on sharing intelligence for a joint strategy of counter terrorism. Indo-Russia relations are backed by a popular as well as an economic consensus in both the countries. Indo-Russian relations are steeped in history and are holistic as they cover economic, social, geostrategic interests. As far as Russia is concerned, it might appear that there is some strategic shift. But Russia has been pushed into that position. In reality, Russia knows that India is still their most reliable ally. They have no conflict of interest or anxiety about India as they do about others. India was instrumental in the construction of a multipolar International system. This system has benefitted India and Russia, not to speak of others like China. A heavy responsibility is cast upon the shoulders of both India and Russia to carry this mission forward.

The paper *' Indo-Soviet Economic Relations'* of ***R. V. R. Chandrasekhara Rao*** has focused how the economic relation between India and Soviet Russia evolved by different treaty and those treaty led to Indo-Soviet cooperation in trade and industrial development. Indo-Soviet economic connections were not only pledges of extensive economic aid, but have gone to the extent of dovetailing its Plan, the product of a highly centralized planning structure and process, with that of India. Nothing short of shedding holy orthodoxy is involved in this marriage between the instruments of "scientific socialism" and "popular socialism." Even more instructive is the point that this change signifies the impact of political and diplomatic realities on economic relations. The implementation of the Treaty goals for economic cooperation has already occasioned some new thinking on 'the Indian side about forging structural links with the Soviet Union. Dovetailing and integration of plans under bilateral agreements to secure cooperation in specific fields was in principle not far away from the then COMECON norms, for the preparation and finalization of the Five Year Plans by the Soviet Union and other Eastern European countries are done after detailed consultation among the parties. It is clear that the Indo-Soviet Joint! Commission is expected to undertake a similar job in the fields chosen for mutual cooperation. Even if full membership in the then COMECON did not come about, close and special type of cooperation between India and the COMECON was visualised.

R. G. Gidadhubli's paper '**India's Exports to Russia: Complexities and Contradictions**' analyzed Indo-Russia trade relation in 90's. Indo-Russian trade turnover shows nearly two-fold increase in 1994 and 1995. The four item Tea, Tobacco, Soya meal and medicines were imported by Russia. Both Indian and Russian policy- makers may feel satisfied with this improved performance in trade volume as compared to the steep decline in trade in 1992-93 consequent upon the disintegration of the USSR. With the economic liberalization taking place simultaneously in the two countries, the potential for expanding trade between India and Russia is very considerable. The author also point out several complexities and contradictions in fully exploiting India's potentialities for increasing exports to Russia. He suggested setting up of a joint venture by India and Russia is banking and finance for promoting bilateral economic relations.

'Indo-Russian Trade and Economic Cooperation: the Way Ahead' written by **Arun Mohanty** has pointed out that the large economies of India and Russia are complementary in nature in spite of infrastructural bottlenecks and they have also enjoyed excellent political relationship. Both the nations have huge potential for growth of bilateral trade. Indo-Russian defence cooperation has played an important part of growing strategic partnership between the two countries. The author has also discussed about the significant annual rate growth of both economies which is treated as potentiality of bilateral trade of India and Russia. In the 21st century, along with traditional commodities intellectual rights for innovative technologies must become a significant point of the bilateral Russian-Indian cooperation market.

'Russia's Resurgence: Global-Regional Threats and Opportunities' paper of **Aymen Ijaz** has focused rise and fall of great powers in world politics. The paper intends to focus how and why Russia is resurging on the political stage after its decline, with a special focus on its relationship with neighbouring Ukraine. Historical background, domestic compulsions, economic and security concerns, and leadership are the important factors. It suggests a way forward for Russia in the prevailing challenges and changing global political environment. It concludes that Russia has revived itself as a powerful state, but in the current scenario the concept of a unipolar world has been replaced by a multipolar world. The study concludes that while Russia is facing challenges in re-establishing itself as a major global player, hard power politics is not the way forward. Instead, the regime in Moscow should focus on enhancing its position and power through economic alliances and partnerships.

The article **'Indo-Russian Relations and the Emerging International Power Structure'** of **Rajan Kumar** pointed out that the relationship between India and Russia goes much beyond the sphere of mere bilateral relations. The partnership assumes special significance because it is based not simply on mutual economic, cultural and political interactions but it is a reflection of mutual perception of international power structure and the existing balance of power. It seeks to create its own niche in that structure and works to face the threat and opportunities provided by that structure cohesively. This in turn makes it imperative for any discussion on Indo-Russia relation to locate it against the backdrop of the emerging global and regional politics. The paper begins by describing the unfolding of international power structure that has a profound impact on the foreign policy of both India and Russia.

Acharya (1992), in his article **"India and the Super powers during Nehru era"** has discussed India's closeness with Soviet Union as well as criticism for this relation during Nehru's pursuit of the policy of Non-alignment. As the main theme of the article is to examine how USA and other powers like Britain had tried to pressurize India contrary to its national interest Soviet Union remained steady in its friendly relation with India and proved during Chinese invasion that the conflict with one communist power did not mean conflict with other communist countries. After that India's Foreign policy became more pragmatic and less doctrinaire. One important thing is while that non-alignment did not mean that India would have same type of relation with every power. First India had close relation with Britain for economic and military assistance but this relation did not continue for long time because Nehru wanted to play world role. Gradually India and the then USSR became two great friends.

Yadav's paper '**India as rising power: opportunities and challenges**' have explained the operational dynamics of International politics. World is polarized as unipolar, bipolar and multipolar by different major powers and regional powers in International system for their national interest. India has to attain the status of rising power with earned high moral posture in the comity of nations. Economically, India has registered good progress by building bridges through the active participation in regional groupings like EU, ASEAN, BRICS, and SAARC etc. He has also focused India's potentiality to be considered as an important power in the international system along with imperativeness for policy makers with proper perspective and skilful diplomatic maneuvering.

India and Russia in a Changing World written by **Rajen Harshe** has pointed out difficulties to understand the International relations in the changing global system and its effect on India and Russia. The author nicely analyzed the post cold war world and process of globalization. The phenomenon of globalization is pregnant with immense possibilities of homogenization. It might as well boil down to the export of lifestyles or world views of the stronger states to the weaker states. Thus, people around the world might appear depressingly similar in their choices in different spheres of life. However, homogenization need not be confused with abolition of differentiation in power. On the contrary, globalization will provide a new context for power rivalries by providing wider horizons for political action and throw up new set of values, opportunities and alliances. This would qualitatively change the modes of operation of power.

The author emphasized that the Indo-Russian economic ties had been undergoing a phase of transition characterised by the decline in Indo-Russian trade. Indeed, the post-Soviet Russia has been keen on strengthening trade relations with states such as Germany, Italy, Japan and China. Indo- Russian trade became almost negligible from the Russian side by certain problems pertaining to rupee-ruble exchange as well as the modes of working out India's debt repayment to former Soviet Union. But it has been resolved while planning out the Indo-Russian trade arrangements.

Military cooperation between Indo-Russia was in the growing stage. In fact, the post-Soviet Russia has inherited the Soviet repute for producing sophisticated weapons, frontline fighters and strike aircraft such as Su-27, Su-30 and MiG-31. Due to Russian assistance, India has been able to produce a small number of MiG aircraft and upgrade over 1,000 of its 172 tanks. The two countries have also promoted joint production of S-30 BK bombers.

Indo-Russian Relations: Putin's Visit in Perspective by **P. L. Dash** throws light on the Putin's visit on October, 2000 which set the tone for a new beginning in the relationship witnessing the signing of 11 agreements. These agreements marked a substantive improvement in mutual understanding. Russia and India are 'marketising' and globalising in their own ways; both are reforming their economies in a unique fashion, both have a common approach to vital issues of international concern, both have an incredible blend of understanding on destabilising issues such as international and cross-border terrorism, narcotic trafficking, Islamic extremism, arms smuggling and a host of other issues facing their neighbourhood. It seems Indo-Russian relations are once again beginning to bloom. Here the author has emphasized not Indo-Russia bilateral relation only but strategic partnership, also embracing India, China and Russia in a trilateral security arrangement. Moscow-Beijing-New Delhi axis has also been given importance by the author.

Shaumyan's manuscript entitled '***Russian-Indian Bilateral Cooperation'*** highlighted the top priority issues on the bilateral agenda between India and Russia. Russia and India attach a lot of importance to their interaction in the energy sector, which embraces the construction and modernisation of hydroelectric and thermal power plants. The Soviet Union made a substantial contribution in the formation of India's infrastructure at the very outset of that process. Bilateral collaboration between the Soviet and Indian scientific communities was initiated at the level of individual projects, such as the creation of a vaccine against poliomyelitis. India and Russia are particularly interested in seeking long-term cooperation arrangements with regard to nuclear power plant development programmes. Both Russia and India have been moving along towards building up more open, competitive economies integrated with the global system. Russia is helping India in the context of Medicine, Electronic Materials, Information Technologies, Biotechnologies, Aircraft Building, Space Exploration, Military-technology etc. which are the main thrust area of mutual Cooperation.

The work **'India-Russia Strategic Partnership Common Perspectives'** Edited *by* **P. Stobdan** contains several in-depth research papers presented at the two-day dialogue. The issues covered in book are thematic in nature with perspectives from both Russia and India written by individual authors. This has focused on traditional Indo-Russia relation in general and the military-technical relation in particular. The bilateral relationship has continued through international vicissitude and to remain important in years to come. In the context of the issue of Kashmir, Russia's diplomatic support to India is crucial. The changes in the global economies have widened the opportunities for India and Russia to look at new convergence of interests. Moreover, the economies of both the countries are complementary to each other. India has emphasized constructive and mutual cooperation with member countries of SAARC, ASEAN, BRICS and other economic organizations of the World but not at the cost of old friendship with Russia. India and Russia strategic partnership needs to be fostered in the changing international system. Traditionally, both countries have favoured a rule based international order and both nations have upheld the notion of a multi-polar world. India's globalizing service industries and corporate sectors can help diversify the Russian economy and develop bilateral trade. In international politics the author wished that India should not forget its old and time-tested strategic partner, as the traditionally strong US-Pakistan and China-Pakistan nexus still persists.

'India and Russia: Allies in the International Political System' paper of ***Anuradha M. Chenoy*** has focused hegemonic power of the super power i.e US. Both nations Russia and India have a common vision of creation of a multi-polar world with the support of co-existence of multiple powers and possibilities in the international system. Consequently Multi-polarity broadens the concept of security. The author also emphasized that Russia, India, China and others can engage seriously with the US and all other powers, and seek to strengthen this relation while maintaining an independent foreign policy. Both India and Russia have expressed concern that the international coalition against the non state actors is imperative. Both the countries are important for each other in global politics especially to check the hegemonic world order.

Das Kundu has analyzed the '***economic growth*** of ***India and Russia and how Indo-Russia relation gain a new self-confidence'*** in her Paper entitled India-Russia Relationship: Past, Present & Future. As rising economic powers, both India and Russia are playing an increasingly larger role on the world stage. The two countries share the goal of creating a multipolar world. This paper has also thrown light on export and import of military product from Russia to India. The author has pointed out the past, present and future of Russia-India relation. India's trusted strategic partner is destined to play a vital role in ensuring India's energy security in the coming decades.

The paper **'India and Russia: Reassessing the Time-Tested Ties'** written by **B.M. Jain** mainly studies the various phases in their relationship since the Cold War period within the theoretical perspectives of Cold War geopolitics, Gorbachev's "new political thinking" paradigm and Putin's pragmatic policy approach. The author has drawn attention to the post-Stalin leadership in Moscow slowly coming to recognize India's geopolitical importance within the contours of its broad strategic framework. India's special place in and contribution to the non-aligned movement was a strong incentive for Moscow to cultivate its relationship with India. Geopolitically, India's non-aligned policy far better suited the Soviet Union's strategic interests in a bipolar world, since it presented the newly independent Afro-Asian countries with an alternative to joining US-led military alliances. Indo-Russia bilateral ties are likely to meet with greater success, especially in the defence and strategic fields, than during the Indo-Soviet friendship era. The defence ties of both countries are not restricted to the mere buyer-seller relationship. Russia and India has been neither clashing territorial ambitions nor conflicting political and strategic interests, unlike India and China.

Dubey's article **'Indo-(Soviet) Russian Relations'** has analysed the Indo-Soviet economic relation and bilateral agreement under different leadership of both the countries. The trade relation between India and Russia has also been emphasized. The Soviet Union emerged as the largest trading partner of India as well as the biggest destination of India's exports from the 1980's. A large part of the goodwill and friendship of the Russian people, which was cultivated during the period of Indo-Soviet relationship, still survives, though in a dormant form, partly because of the lack of energetic effort by India to revitalize and draw upon it for fostering cooperation between the two countries. The agenda for the strategic partnership between the two countries is being continuously widened, depending upon the need to reach understanding or forge common positions on developing strategic issues. An increase in the two-way flow of investment, undertaking joint projects and joint collaboration for the development of innovative technologies in the civilian sector can have the effect of propelling the trade between the two nations to new heights.

The book **India and ASEAN in the 21st Century** authored by **Sanjay Ambatkar (2002)** has focused on economic scenario and trade perspective of India and ASEAN in comparison with World. Despite financial turbulence in the region, the member states are high in spirit to achieve the goal of ASEAN Economic Region by the year 2020. He has analyzed various dimensions of economic cooperation between India and ASEAN and the emerging trend concerning trade and investment. In the context of trade and foreign investment the period 1980s and 1990s played an important role in shaping rapid economic development of the ASEAN-5. Until China arrived on the map of world FDI, the ASEAN-5, especially Singapore was the most favorable investment destination among developing countries. In the present time Indian investors have reposed faith on ASEAN and looked for mutual market for them. Here the author discussed a very good trade scenario in 90s and especially after the initiation of 'Look East Policy' among India and ASEAN member countries. Singapore share in total export of ASEAN-5 to India in 1992-98 is more than 50%.Thus during 1985-98 Singapore emerged as the most important trading partner of

India (followed by Malaysia). This trend is also continuing at present.

Raghuramapatruni's (2012) work on **India's Trade with the ASEAN: Realities and prospects** have focused on the trade reciprocity index between India and ASEAN countries. The slow growth of SAARC and the disintegration of the USSR have led to bring possibility for India to create new partners. In 1992 with the leadership of P.V.Narasimharao LEP initiated the process of reviving India's economic partnership with ASEAN nations. Here the author highlighted the relations between India and ASEAN (Indonesia, Singapore, Malaysia, Philippines and Thailand). India and ASEAN have developed people-to-people interactions involving exchange programmes. India's trade in comparison with the world trade and analysis of India's aggregate exports to and imports from ASEAN member Countries has expanded. The author finally expressed that the ASEAN and India, together can be the catalyst for the region's peace and prosperity.

Mohanty(2012) in his book ***Foreign Policy of India in the 21st Century*** has focused on India's relations with the major powers i.e. US, Russia, China and with countries of South East Asia. Historical background of India and America during the time of independence and cold war has been highlighted. He has taken note of the geopolitical situation in the Indian sub-continent which changed permanently in India's favour. It was no longer possible for the US to maintain the artificial parity between India and Pakistan. The equation of India-USSR and America –Pakistan has also been emphasized in global changing environment. The close ties of US –Pakistan did not allow the growth of the bilateral ties between India and US. The end of cold war and the disintegration of the Soviet Union altered much of the international alliances structures of the cold war period. The disappearance of the Soviet Union form the global strategic framework created the necessity for India to engage with the west and the US in a more effective manner. The author also focused the US-India security ties as providing an alleged counterbalance to growing Chinese influence in Asia. The most important intimate phase of Indo-Soviet Union relations has also been discussed which is based on continuity, trust , mutual understanding. India and Russia cooperation is not limited to a buyer-seller relationship but includes joint research and development training, service contacts including joint exercises. India and South East Asia relation has also got boost after the Look East policy (LEP) which is present Act east policy; it is also emphasized by the above author. The first phase of the LEP saw India establish institutional linkages with the regional organizations. By taking advantage of Myanmar as a land bridge to SEA, India hopes to transform the North East from a security burden in to a land of economic opportunity. India's relation with Individual nations of ASEAN has been taken up separately.

'India's Foreign Policy in 21st century: Challenges Ahead' by **Kamboj** brought out that there is greater cooperation among nations and new models of global engagement with India in the era of globalisation. India is also determined to work with neighbors especially SEA nations. India has expanded its defense cooperation with Vietnam against the Chinese assertiveness in the disputed South China Sea. India's developmental priorities emphasized its relations with the major powers and our Asian neighbours. India's vision for the 21st century includes seeking political stability, economic modernization and regional integration of the region.

'India's Defence Diplomacy in South East Asia' authored by **Pankaj Kumar Jha** focused on India's defence diplomacy in Southeast Asia which aims to accommodate concerns of its neighbours and wants to project its benign role in the region but, of late, the defence diplomacy has China containment strategy also. However, India needs a structured approach in its strategic planning and defence diplomacy while dealing with Southeast Asian countries. In the end, what matters is national security and strategic interest, not the morality rhetoric.The enhanced Indian naval profile in Southeast Asia serves several objectives. One is to strengthen India's so-called "Look East" policy that is intended in part to balance China's influence in the eastern Indian Ocean region (Indonesia, Malaysia, Thailand, Myanmar, etc.) and in western Southeast Asia.

Palit in his paper **India's Act East Policy and Implications for Southeast Asia** has pointed out that the present status of Look East Policy. In 2014 India-ASEAN summit in Myanmar the Indian Prime Minister Narendra Modi declared the promotion of India's "Look East Policy" (LEP) to a more action-oriented "Act East" strategy. India's growing posturing over the tensions in the South China Sea can be taken as an example of the "multi-alignment" likely to characterize its Act East policy. The Act East strategy is expected to deepen India's engagement with Southeast Asia on a variety of issues. The wider geographic scope of the strategy and its extension beyond Southeast Asia has probably been motivated by the realization on the part of India that a strategic vision for Southeast Asia is not exclusive of a similar vision for East Asia and the Asia-Pacific. Similarly, strategic views of the latter cannot be constructed without corresponding visions of Southeast Asia.

Ganapathi's paper on ***'Look East - Act East' Dimension of India's Foreign Policy*** has highlighted how the nation's economic policy and foreign policy are interlinked and the transformation of India's look east to Act east policy and it s importance in global politics. The scope of India's Look East philosophy was expanded from a mere trade and economic engagement to include issues of strategic and geopolitical significance. India has excellent relations with Singapore, Thailand, Malaysia and other ASEAN members. While India's interaction with Indonesia has been productive, India needs to give some more thrust to its partnership with this important ASEAN member.

This paper basically focused on the involvement of individual states in regional organizations and their aims to change the global system. Nehru had long been an admirer of the Soviet economic system, and while he was not drawn to the concept of a one-party state, had an affinity with the socialist system of the Soviet Union. The once close relationship was further strained by the political distance that India consciously kept from the newly formed ASEAN, which it saw as a reincarnation of the Southeast Asia Treaty Organization and American conspiracy to use Southeast Asian states to serve its Cold War designs in the region. Author also focused on economic liberalization and the importance of look east policy for Indo-ASEAN relationship and emphasized on Pan-Asianism. The old balance of power approach must give way to a greater acceptance of multi-polarity, not only globally but in Asia as well." In other words, India would want to keep its options open so as to preserve autonomy of action as it relates to the US, China, or Russia.

The book **Foreign Policy of India and Asia-Pacific** edited **by K.Raja Reddy(2012)** provides valuable inputs of facts and ideas about Asia-pacific region. Some of the articles among those have focused India's bilateral relations with China and strategic partnership with Indonesia & Vietnam. India's growing engagement with South East Asia shows that India's foreign policy is geared to meet the demands of the interdependent world whose catch words are peace and development. The ASEAN countries too are looking for an opportunity to take full advantage of India's economic reforms and the opening up of the Indian economy. The International environment too is propitious enough for India and ASEAN, to resume a reinvigorated partnership for which our Look East Policy and ASEAN's Look West Policy provided the impetus. The emerging relationship is based on convergences and the imperatives of profound post cold war strategic, economic and political changes underway. The progress and rapid growth of relations between India and ASEAN depends on peace and stability in our extended neighbourhood. This unique partnership may help in a greater way to establish multipolarism in the world.

Pattnaik in his article '**Putin - Modi Summit at Sochi: New Informality in India-Russia Relations**' has highlighted There are qualitative changes in the nature of defence relations between the two states. From being a market of Soviet arms, today both are jointly producing military hardware and intend to sell it to third countries. The BrahMos Missile System and the licensed production in India of the SU-30 aircraft and T-90 tanks are examples of such new trajectory of cooperation. Russia agreed to supply latest weapons like S-400 air defence systems and construct frigates. Both sides also agreed to form a joint venture to manufacture Ka-226T helicopters in India. He added that India still uses Russian origin tanks, aircraft, helicopters, aircraft carrier, ammunition and other systems. However, programmes such as the joint development or outright purchase of the Fifth Generation Fighter Aircraft and Multi-role Transport Aircraft, as also the up-gradation of the Su-30 MKI aircraft, are the new ones that would take the defence relations to a new level. He specifically mentions that the beginning of this century reveals that emerging major regional players like Russia, China and India are feeling uncomfortable with the unipolar world order and unilateralism that was being pursued by America and its allies in the 1990s.

Rahul Bedi's Paper **'Moscow looking East to counter U.S power'** points out that aided considerably by anti-US feeling in SEA, Russia sold its multirole fighters to Malayasia and Indonesia. Officials commented that Kualalumpur decision to buy the Russian fighters would enhance India's strategic and business interest in SEA as it is expected to provide training and servicing to the royal Malayasian Air force for its new Su-30's. The author has quoted Dr. Alex Vaskin of the Indo-Russia's strategic forum as India having acted as a gateway for Russia's arms sales to SEA.

Acharya and Mohanty have pointed out in the paper entitled '**Indo-Russian cooperation in South East Asia: A move towards multipolar world**' that when drastic changes took place of former USSR in terms of ideology, polity and economy, Russia emerged as the major inheritor of the disintegrated communist system. Relation with India remained a low key affair in the foreign policy calculus of Russia. The resurgent Russia, however, is looking towards its friendship with India and both are active in South East Asia the region which has come out with added luster during the globalization period. India, Russia and China are emerging powers at the global level and their relations have the potentiality to check the unipolar world and are leading towards multipolarity. They have added that a country like Malayasia has bought Russian Mig 29 fighters and Mi-17 helicopters, after studying India's experience with these aircraft. Other SEA states like Indonesia and Vietnam are toeing a similar line.

Evelyn Goh, in his research paper entitled **'Great Powers And Southeast Asian Regional Security Strategies: Omni-Enmeshment, Balancing And Hierarchical Order'** has pointed out that the small and medium-sized states in Southeast Asia have undergone significant geo-strategic changes with the end of the Cold War and the rise of China. There has been a lively debate over the last decade about whether these countries would balance against or bandwagon with China, and how their relations with the other major powers in the region would change. Recent works that argue against the simple dichotomy of balancing versus bandwagoning are correct in asserting that Southeast Asian countries do not want to choose between the two major powers, the U.S. and China. It finds that instead of merely adopting tactical or time-buying policies; key Southeast Asian states have actively tried to influence the shaping of the new regional order. It argues that key Southeast Asian states in fact have (a) distinct conceptualizations of two main pathways to order in the region – Omni-enmeshment of major powers and complex balance of influence; and (b) a concrete vision of the preferred power distribution outcome, which is a hierarchical regional order.

Arunrat Jinda *examines the foreign policy of Russia in the Southeast Asia which emphasize* Russia's quest for regional influence especially cooperation with ASEAN nations and the strategic benefits of both Russia and ASEAN. A solid relationship could provide a greater balance in Russia's Asia policy, supporting the multipolarity that ensures continuing Russian influence in world affairs in the face of American predominance. In the 21st century the vista of Russia in Southeast Asia will build up. Russia has started re-engaging with Southeast Asian countries Under Putin's policy, with low publicity. Development of a cooperation of Russia in Southeast Asia infringes on interests of the world in wider structure for cooperation in political and economic to the sphere.

Rangsimaporn, (2009) argues that Southeast Asia is important for Russia because the region presents opportunities for Russia to play a more influential role there and in East Asia more generally. Improved relations with Asian states accorded well with Primakov's vision of multipolarity in which many centers of power lay in Asia, some of which shared Russian concerns over U.S. unilateral-ism. This article looks at how Russia perceives Southeast Asia and how this relates to the realization of Russian aspirations to be a great power and to be *perceived* as such. This endeavor has been increasingly focused under President Vladimir Putin and is reinforced by rising fuel prices that bolster the state's relentless economic growth and increasingly confident, self-assertive foreign policy. A solid relationship could provide a greater balance in Russia's Asia policy, bolstering the multipolarity that ensures continuing Russian influence in world affairs in the face of American predominance.

Stephen Blank has focused the changing dimension of Russia and Southeast Asia relation in an age where geo-economics is supposed to have supplanted geo-strategy, a bilateral or multilateral relationship between states where vital security interests are not present, like this one, should reflect particularly strongly a pattern of more or less rationally conceived growing economic mutuality. His paper 'Is There A Future For Russian Relations With Southeast Asia?' has emphasized the "economization" of Russian foreign policy should be particularly noticeable vis-a-vis Southeast Asia precisely because no vital security issues color Russia's ties to those nations.

The book ***American Hegemony and the trilateral commission*** authored by ***Gill*** found some theoretical perspectives of hegemony in general and about hegemony of America in particular. He defines the concept of hegemony in the realist sense. Like world systems theorists, realists define hegemony in terms of the predominance of one nation in the inter-state system, equating hegemony with domination fastened in an asymmetrical allocation of military and economic potentialities. The Weberian view of power has also been emphasized here. America's rise to hegemony was not only partly caused by a relatively efficient economic system capable of absorbing foreign investment during the 19thcentury, but also its unique ability to attract large quantities of skilled and unskilled labour.

Rosemary Foot, S.Neil MacFarlane and Michael Mastanduno's book entitled ***US hegemony and International Organisations*** has focused American multilateralism and multilateral security has also been perused. This is because a part of the theme of the research work relates to a move towards the multi-polar world. 'US Hegemony and International Organizations' brings together a range of leading scholars to examine this crucial phenomenon. Its aims are two-fold: to describe and explain US behaviour in and towards a wide range of significant global and regional institutions; and secondly to examine the impact of US behavior on the capacity of each organization to meet its own objectives.

The main focus of the work ***Return of the Dragon US-China Relations in the 21st Century*** edited by ***Danny Paau, Herbert Yee*** is US strategic interest and US's relations with other countries of the World. The Chinese scholar Yang Chengxu, has been found to stress the importance of constructing a sound trilateral relationship between China, Russia and India. As China, Russia and Russia and India have established strategic partnership and all advocate political multi-polarity and economic globalization. The three nations have a lot of common interests being more oriented towards a multi-polar world and thereby they want to check pax-Americana.

Another book entitled ***India's relations with Russia and China-A new Phase*** edited by ***M Rasgotra & V D Chopra*** has pointed out India's relation with China in the Post-Cold war period based on empirical studies in the end of the present century is of far reaching importance both for Indian and Foreign experts. These three countries have a large number of common problems. Therefore strengthening of their political, economic and cultural relations through interaction with each other has its own significance. The center of gravity of the world power in the end of the present century has already shifted from Europe to the Asia-Pacific region. The actors like US, Japan, China & Russia are already engaged in a power struggle in this region.

The book ***India-China relations Politics of Resources, Identity and authority in Multipolar World order*** by ***Jagannath P Panda*** has focused the enduring and emerging complexities in India and China relations. The rise of India and China as two major economic and political actors in both regional and global politics necessitates an analysis of not only their bilateral ties but also the significance of their regional and global pursuits. This book looks at the nuances and politics that the two countries attach to multilateral institutions and examines how they receive, react to and approach each other's presence and upsurge. Another important thing is that India's previous Look East Policy was advanced further with the December 2012 India-ASEAN commemorative summit marking 20 years of India's association with ASEAN and the 10th Anniversary of India-ASEAN Summit level partnership, to upgrade the bilateral ties to a 'strategic partnership'. The crux of this Commemorative Summit was an evolving security understanding between the two sides, mainly on the aspect of maritime cooperation. In East Asia, India enjoys a good thrust of 'Strategic Partnership' with Japan, South Korea and ASEAN, the last being the most important. A prime aspect of India's defence diplomacy with ASEAN member states is its maritime approach with the region. ASEAN members like Myanmar, Singapore, Thailand, Malaysia and Indonesia are important to India's maritime diplomacy in the north-east Indian Ocean, where India has usually maintained its maritime authority. The book argues that coexistence between India and China in this multipolar world order is possible, but that it is limited to a medium-term perspective, given the constraints of identity complexities and global aspirations these two rising powers are pursuing. It goes on to discuss how their search for energy resources, quest to uphold their own identity as developing powers, and engagement in balance-of-power politics to exert authority on each other's presence, are some elements that guide their non-cooperative relationship.

The significance of the book entitled '**Russia China Relations: Relevance for India'** by Jyotsna Bakshi of IDSA is that the relations between Russia and China - one of the largest states in the world from point of view of territory and the other from point of view of population - have always impacted the course of the global and regional geopolitics. No wonder, the course of Sino-Soviet relations has always evoked keen interest in the major capitals of the world. From the Indian perspective, the study of Sino-Russian relations and their implications for India is of particular importance. India, Russia and China are the three largest countries of the Eurasian continent. Moscow-Beijing relationship at any given point of time - whether cooperative or antagonistic - has always tended to have profound implications for Indian policy towards both. The narrative of Russia China relations in the present book focuses on the contemporary post-Soviet period. Beset by numerous domestic problems and external challenges, new Russia has sought to follow a 'balanced' policy towards the West as well as the East in a bid to create a conductive environment for the economic and military revival of the country. Indeed, both Moscow and Beijing have sought to improve their bilateral ties in the post-Cold War period without constraining the freedom of the sides in the pursuit of a flexible, multi-vector policy.

The article entitled '**The Lonely Superpower'** by **Samuel P. Huntington** published in foreign affairs draw the attention to the fact that the uni-polar moment dawned in 90's. He further pointed out that even old allies stubbornly resisted American demands, while many other nations viewed U.S. policy and ideals as openly hostile to their own. Washington was blind to the fact that it no longer enjoyed the dominance it had at the end of the Cold War. It must relearn the game of international politics as a major power, not a superpower, and make compromises. U.S. policymaking should reflect rational calculations of power rather than a wish list of arrogant, unilateralist demands.

Donette Murray's book entitled 'Multipolarity in the 21st Century: A New World Order' look for debate on power and polarity in the twenty-first century, both by assessing the likelihood of US decline and by analysing what each of the so-called 'rising powers' can do. American supremacy continues to generate intense discuss about the nature, quality and sustainability of US power. At the same time, significant developments in four rising powers - China, Russia, India and the European Union – have provoked analysts to ask whether multipolarity is a realistic prospect. Multipolarity in the 21st Century assesses the likelihood of a multipolar world developing, either by a marked US decline and or by the ability of these putative 'rivals' to continue to rise to the level necessary to be credibly considered a superpower.

India, China, Russia intricacies of an Asian Triangle edited by **Gilles Boquerat &Frederic Grare** has focused on the triangle of Asian bringing together to India, China, Russia in the end of 90's as strategic partner and attracted public attention. The east-west, the Sino-Soviet and the Sino-Indian cold wars had receded in popular memory and a triangular equation gained enough credibility to deserve closer examination. The validity of an Asian triangle remains to be substantiated. Here the question of Author is 'has this geometric figure a life of its own, Can it further the cause of multipolarity or is it just a tool for its constituents to improve their standing vis-à-vis the US in a unipolar world? In this book Kanti Bajpai's worked on Confidence building between India, China and Russia and intends to explore the mutual relation for international security. China and India already have a formal confidence building process going back to the early 1990's. India and Russia do not really need confidence building: there is very little prospect of conflict between them. China and Russia have signed a number of agreements in recent years and are collaborating in various areas. India China and Russia can do some sensible things together in the military and geopolitical realm.

In the publication **'Russian-Chinese relations: past, present and future' by Vladimir Paramonov and Aleksey strokov** have pointed out that the history of relations between the two countries is characterised by periods of rapprochement interspersed with periods of cool, if not tense, relations. Secondly, the present close relationship between Russia and China in the political sphere and military technology area is not providing sufficient stimulus to economic relations between the two countries, which are confined to trade (comprising mainly the exchange of Russian raw materials for Chinese manufactured goods) and hardly involve industry and investment. The most likely development, seen from today's perspective, is the gradual economic absorption of the Asiatic part of Russia by China. This scenario could not only lead to conflict between the two states, but could affect Eurasia as a whole (half of which is made up of Russia and China).

Nandan Unnikrishnan & Uma Purushothaman in Observer Research Foundation have highlighted that in a rapidly-changing world where new powers and fresh alliances are emerging, Russia-China relations will form a key component in determining the evolution of the balance of power in the world. There is increasing convergence between Russia and China on several global issues.

Moscow and Beijing openly coordinate positions on these issues, particularly in the UN Security Council. They are also engaged in multilateral fora such as RIC, SCO, and BRICS, and see such an engagement as one way of strengthening a multipolar world in which they are key players as well as a platform to present an alternative viewpoint to the Western-dominated global discourse.

The present study is likely to be improvement on the earlier works because it takes in to account the relation between India and Russia in general and specifically in the context of Southeast Asia and seeks to explore how that relation can be a counter to the dominant influence of America in the region. In particular it wants to study the specific economic cooperation between India and Russia in the context of countries of SEA. The area of cooperation in specific products is further sought to be identified. Review of the existing work shows that there is availability of study material with regard to

(i) Soviet Russia relations

(ii) Indo-ASEAN relations

(iii) India, Russia. China relations in carving out a multipolar world etc.

But this work is an improvement on all previous works in the sense that it focuses Indo-Russian cooperation in the globalization context especially with regard to their trade and other relations with South East Asian countries. Moreover it not only examines the issue of a multipolar world attempted by the trio of India, China and Russia but also how India seeks to balance China in the context of South East Asia. It seeks to take an in-depth view of Indo-Russian cooperation in South East Asia from that perspective.

Chapter - 2

India's Relations with South East Asia

If one analyzes the international·system from cold war to present time, one notices lot of changes having taken place in world political system. The end of bipolarity has resulted in the domination of world affairs by the single state which is economically, industrially and military strong i.e. US. Over the years it gave way to multipolarity. The end of cold war, the inauguration of economic liberalisation and growing significance of geo-economic factors led to fundamental reorientation in India's Foreign policy. India started reviving its traditional relation with SEA nations for the economic prosperity and regional cooperation and stability.

India's Relations with South East Asia (Cold War to Present Time)

India and Southeast Asia relations have deep historical roots. It impacted cultural, economic, and political field in their mutual relation. But India had lost its regional influence due to colonialism. Still India tried to rebuild its traditional role in the region after gaining independence. The South East Asia was theatre of major power rivalry in the cold war era. During those days India shield away from close interaction with the region because of its non-aligned policy. But during Rajiv Gandhi's tenure India conveyed its willingness to be associated with the region. It must not be glossed over, however, that India established its influence in the Southeast Asian region during the 1950s by supporting the Indonesian struggle for independence and involving itself in the Indo-china crisis in the 1960s.

The initial seeds of Look East policy can be said to have been sown even before India became free from the colonial yoke. During the period of globalisation, Look East policy turned out to be of strategic importance for both India and SEA. The policy is about reaching out to our civilisational neighbours in South East Asia and East Asia.

India and SEA: Various Phases

As an old civilisation of worshippers of the Sun God, India has always been looking east. The worship of the Sun God is perfectly manifest at the sun temple of Konark. It represents the Sun God standing in the Time's Winged Chariot urging the team of seven horses with which he blazes his way through the heaven. Truly speaking in this temple the language of man is defeated by the language of the stone. The old civilisational ties may be reinforced during the present era of globalisation. The relations of India with the east can be said to have passed through four stages or better known as four waves. These are: (i) Historical or pre-colonial, (ii) Colonial, (iii) Post colonial and (iv) Contemporary.

FIRST WAVE

The geographic location of India is such that she is the pivot of western, southern and the South-East Asia. The past has witnessed cultural contact between India and different parts of Asia.

ANCIENT INDIA

No doubt India and South East Asia had trading relation with each other in ancient period. Dravidian kingdoms on India's southeast coast, of which the Chola kingdom was most important, dominated shipping across the Bay of Bengal. During this period, the first Hindu empire prospered, based wholly on cultural and philosophical contacts with India. No military missions were initiated and there were no wars, except Indian emperor Rajendra Chola's periodic encroachment into the Srivijiya Empire in Malaya and Indonesia in the 10th and 11th century. Indian merchants were the first outsiders to seek out the wealth of Southeast Asia, known as the "land of gold" but more deservedly famous for spices. Indian traders, adventurers, teachers and priests continued to be the dominating influence in South East Asia until about A.D. 1500, and Indians often ruled the earliest states in these regions. Hinduism and Buddhism both spread to these states from India and for many centuries existed there with mutual toleration. Eventually the states of the mainland became mainly Buddhist.

Cultural and Economic Contact

The religious and cultural synthesis of the two major systems namely, Hinduism and Buddhism took place and the imprint is found even today. The advent of Buddhism and its unfolding in Southeast Asia is a glorious chapter in itself and reminds one of the ancient and historic links between India and Southeast Asia. The tremendous popularity of Ramayan in the Buddhist heartland of Southeast Asia, may be, bears unmistakable impressions of this interface. Thus, there is evidence of a shared legacy in the myth and legends, religion and culture, crafts and arts, the language the people speak and the adventures business and trade that took place centuries ago. Thus, the history of the pre-colonial period suggests that India and ASEAN are no 'awkward strangers' they have been neighbours and good friends in time space and existence for as long as histories can enumerate (Ghosh, 2009). Odisha's annual festival of 'Bali Jatra' symbolises the adventures of innumerable traders who brave rough seas across the Bay of Bengal, Straits of Malacca and South China Sea in pursuit of trade and culture to the eastern shores of the Indian Ocean.

Thus, in the pre-colonial period there is evidence of India's dynamic and extensive relation with its eastern neighbours since the 1st century. The colonial expansion that followed Muslim rule in India disrupted the cultural and commercial links. During colonialism the Second World War engulfed East Asia extensively. A strategic dimension was added by the war to India's links with Southeast Asia.

SECOND WAVE

The Britishers built India as the bastion of their power and influence in Asia that protected their colonial holding as far in the East as possible. This may be characterised as is the second wave of India's Look East Policy when strategic interests were given priority along with the commercial interests as the cost of cultural and civilisational pulls. The legacy of India's colonial sway continues in many subtle ways. It alerts East Asian countries and interested major powers to project and even exaggerate India's possible 'expansionist' and adventurist intention. But there is no evidence to support such intention. It also makes Indian policy-makers conscious about a wider strategic perspective that increases the critical significance of the Indian Ocean and the eastern sea board in its security calculus.

THIRD WAVE

The third wave or the post-colonial period of India's LEP started with the advent of Independence. While working for Asian resurgence, India took into account its neighbours. Nehru convened the Asian relations conference in March 1947 that is even before India got its Independence. Other Leaders of Asian countries accepted Nehru's Pan-Asian vision, specifically his thrust on decolonisation and economic cooperation. He was the architect of independent India's foreign policy, in general and its Asia policy in particular. His vision of a 'Closer union' with the East was moulded by the strength of India's geographical proximity, similarity of historical experiences, cultural identity and economic interest etc. The vast expanse of Indian Ocean and its economic and strategic significance in links with eastern neighbours was not lost sight of by Nehru. Besides the Non-Alignment Movement, communism also impacted India's relations with SEA region. During the Vietnam conflict, India extended support to North Vietnam due to its strong opposition at that time to the United States. While the cold war scenario shaped India's relation with Southeast Asia, given its closeness to the Soviet Union, India also had reasonable ties with Malaysia and was amongst the first countries to accord diplomatic status to Singapore in 1965.

Decolonisation and Indian Policy Makers

Indian policy makers and diplomats forcefully articulated and advocated the cause of decolonisation and development of Asian countries in all possible international forums. Reacting sharply to the Dutch attack on the newly born republic of Indonesia in July 1947, Nehru commented that "the spirit of new Asia will not tolerate such things. However, it must not be glossed over that two centuries of colonisation by the British made India largely Eurocentric in its global outlook for at least three of the five post-independence decades. This led to disproportionate emphasis given to the occident and its concerns, often out of tune with global realities and to the neglect of the Orient, the Far-East, South East, and other parts of Asia. Another factor was the cold war which distorted perspectives in the foreign policy sphere.

Suspicion of Growing Indo-Soviet Partnership among SEA Countries

It is worth mentioning that during the period of cold war, relation between India and SEA could not blossom due to preoccupation of India with Pakistan factor and East-west rivalry. As a result there was the neglect of the LEP. Even during Mrs Gandhi's period India used to be misunderstood by many countries of SEA due to its closeness with former USSR. Countries which were the followers of USA in that region didn't appreciate India's design in collaboration with the then Soviet Union. The conflict between USSR and China, the partial withdrawal of the Americans from Vietnam and normalisation of relations between China and USA also had its impact on the policy of the countries of South East Asia. This provided a good opportunity to India to cultivate better relations with countries of SEA. It can't be denied that India's pro-Soviet tilt in the foreign policy greatly hampered the development of friendly and cooperative relations with the countries of SEA. (Mohanty, 2012) As a result India wasn't taken in to confidence in the formation of ASEAN. But the situation changed after Rajiv Gandhi became the Prime Minister. His visit to Indonesia, Thailand, Myanmar and Vietnam and above all 'ice breaking' visit to China paved the way for better understanding.

With the, integration of Indian economy with the world economy after the collapse of the Soviet Union as the composite state relations of India with the SEA and EA neighbours opened up. The compulsion of the situation was such that India facing economic crisis could no more turn towards Soviet Union for economic help. As a consequence India had to remove the restriction on the trade and appreciated better understanding with EA neighbours. All this led to the LEP becoming more vigorous and focused.

The Region during Cold War

Indian foreign policy during that stage was obsessed with proximity to Soviet Union which in turn caused ups and downs in relations with US, Britain, France, Germany, and Japan. For India, cold war politics intruded too much in to the psyche of foreign policy planner. Indian foreign policy reflected Nehru's vision of the world, that it was divided into two hostile camps led by United States and Soviet Union, both equipped with nuclear warheads, having the potentiality to destroy the world many times over. India's role was to organise and project a "bloc" advocating and promoting peace, with a policy of staying away and not aligning itself with either of the super-powers. It stood opposed to the pacts such as CENTO (Central Treaty Organisation), MEDO (Middle East defence Organisation) and SEATO (Southeast Asia Treaty Organisation) that the United States organised under its military leadership on the grounds that they were the props needed to shore up the Communist bloc and prevent it from further expansion. That was also the justification of the US and its allies to keep Vietnam, Laos and Cambodia from falling to the Communist bloc, an eventuality that was feared would lead to all of Southeast Asian countries falling like dominoes to Communism and possibly to Communist Chinese domination. But for Burma, Cambodia, Laos, Indonesia and North Vietnam, the rest of Southeast Asia had organised since 1967 under the ASEAN being rightly regarded pro-Western, pro-US, anti-Communist and therefore, with suspicion by India. The dichotomy in Southeast Asia continued even after the end of the Vietnam conflict and the establishment of Communist regimes in Cambodia and Laos. Moreover another factor of distortion in India's foreign policy calculation was its relation with neighbour Pakistan. This again led to the effort of India to keep Europe and the West in good humour lest they challenge New Delhi's stand on Kashmir. In spite of this Nehru's effort towards a resurgent Asia and Asian solidarity is commendable. In fact, the leaders of independent India, particularly Nehru, took the lead in launching the third wave by focusing on East Asia as an important part of India's policy of Asian resurgence.

Nehru's Vision (1947-1964)

Thanks to Jawaharlal Nehru and his strong advocacy of the doctrine of Non-alignment there began a substantial degree of interaction between India and the members of the Non-aligned movement. In fact, India developed in the form of Non-alignment an alternative model of pursuing an independent foreign policy for the newly independent countries of the world. India chose to pursue its objective of peace not by joining any military bloc, but by deciding each issue on its merit. India's contact with growing members of the movement enabled it to make friendship with several countries in the region which it had neglected over the years. Accordingly, he put India in the forefront of mobilising international support on issues ranging from Indonesia's freedom struggle and Burma's internal security and stability, to that of peace and freedom of Indo-China states. (Muni, 2011) India had always supported the concept of the Malaysian federation. In South Asian regional setting, India also made efforts to forge closer friendly ties with Nepal, Sri Lanka, and Burma prior to 1962, India's relations which these neighbours were not so good but in the aftermath of the Sino-Indian war, the strategic importance of these neighbours was felt more by India in terms of thwarting future penetration of Chinese influence in these countries. Malaysia (and Singapore) extended diplomatic support to India during the Chinese invasion. India had its difficulties with China from Hindu-chini-bhai-bhai euphoria, relations with China marked all time low in the wake of the 1962 aggression. In the 60s with departure of Nehru from the scene, the only friends India had in Southeast Asia were the three pro-Soviet communist states of North Vietnam, Laos and Cambodia. Relations with other countries of Southeast Asia wouldn't get deep rooted and mutually beneficial since the countries of that region viz. Malaysia, Thailand, Indonesia, Singapore, Philippines were pro-west strongly anti-communist.

• ***Shastri's Era (1964-66)***

This policy was given a major push by Lal Bahadur Shastri who became the Prime Minister of India after Nehru's death in May 1964. Keeping in view the strategic importance of Nepal in India's security of its northern border PM Shastri tried to forge closer relations with this Himalayan Kingdom by negotiating several commercial, trade and political agreements. He also tried to cultivate friendly relation with Burma, a country of extreme strategic significance to India. It is through Burma during World War II the Japanese invaded India's North-eastern States of Nagaland and Manipur. Burma is the only Southeast Asian country which happens to be in India's immediate neighbourhood and which was administratively linked to India (till 1937) under British rule. (Nanda, 2003)

Indira Gandhi's Visualisation (1966-77 and 1980-84)

India's shift in approach towards the region was evident from the fact that the then PM, Indira Gandhi embarked on a visit to Australia, New Zealand, Singapore, and Malaysia in 1968 and Japan and Indonesia in 1969. The Indira Gandhi regime paved the way for the beginning of the period of high-level exchanges between India and the countries in Southeast Asia. She initiated a phase which as far as India's policy towards Southeast Asia was concerned had some notable features. During her visit to Malaysia in June 1968, Mrs Gandhi convened a conference of Indian envoys from South East Asia to explore the possibility of closer Indian economic collaboration with the countries of the region. In fact, trade between India and the five Southeast Asian countries of Thailand, Philippines, Singapore, Indonesia, and Malaysia increased dramatically during the 1970s. However, it is worth noting that India was neither consulted nor briefed about the formation of the association of ASEAN. Individually the small and medium states of South East Asian region cannot exert influence on international relations. While fiercely defending their own national sovereignty and territorial integrity, they are fully aware of the fact that a collective entity like ASEAN would be helpful to them individually and collectively. After a number of false starts in forming sub-regional organisations, they have finally come together to work for ASEAN based on enlightened self-interests and the desire to promote peace and prosperity in Southeast Asia.

India's leanings towards the Soviet Union in international affairs, in spite of its commitment to non-alignment its hostility with China and its strong campaign against American war vis-à-vis North Vietnam cost India heavily in diplomatic terms. It is interesting to draw a parallel between the formation of ASEAN and that of SAARC and India's role in these organisations. It was Bangladesh not India which mooted the idea of formation of SAARC. This is because India didn't take a leading role in the formation of SAARC. The signing of the Indo-Soviet treaty following the outbreak of the Bangladesh war further widened the distance between India and the ASEAN region. The Far Eastern Economic Review penned "in all ASEAN capitals there is uneasiness about the present close relationship between the Soviet Union and India and a growing fear that Moscow and New Delhi might be ganging up on the Southeast Asian countries. India is not liked in Jakarta and there is real concern that Moscow may have well acquiesced in a future Indian sphere of influence in the area as part of its policy of containing China".

Moraji Desai Period (1977-79)

As late as November 1976 YB Chavan, then India's foreign minister, had described South-East Asia and West Asia as important areas apart from India's neighbours. A.B. Vajpayee, the new Indian Foreign Minister, has spoken of the need to strengthen social ties with South-East Asia and to make special diplomatic efforts to rectify the situation caused by India's neglect of this area in the past. Prime Minister Morarji R. Desai has also called for rectification of India's failure to develop intensive trade ties with this region. (Singh, 1978)

FOURTH WAVE

India's Look East Policy can be characterised as on the crest of the fourth wave especially during the Prime ministership of Dr. Manmohan Singh. In this phase the then prime minister called upon India and the East Asia to make the 21st century a truly Asian century. The fourth wave of India's LEP is also credited to the former Prime Minister Narasimha Rao and is said to have been propelled by post cold war imperatives of Indian foreign policy. But this does not take into account the initiative taken by Rajiv Gandhi during the late 80s in reviving India's relation with eastern extended neighbours. During the five years (1985-89) of Rajiv Gandhi's rule there was sudden increase in diplomatic exchanges between India and the countries of SEA.

Rajiv Gandhi Era

The countries like Thailand, Indonesia, Vietnam, and Myanmar were visited by Rajiv Gandhi and also a visit was undertaken by him to China in December 1988. He deputed the minister of state for external affairs, K. Natwar Singh to travel to the capitals of the Southeast Asian countries for thrashing out a resolution of Kampuchean issue. India also hosted a number of Southeast Asian leaders, in return. This attempt to open up to the East was essentially strategically induced. Deng Xiaoping had put China on a dynamic path of economic recovery and was building co-operation with its neighbours by withdrawing China's support to the local communist insurgencies. India also tried to change the course of Sino-Indian relations as Rajiv Gandhi's visit opened discussion on outstanding border disputes as well as bilateral economic co-operation. The message which emerged out of Rajiv's visit to China was to keep conflicts and disagreement on the back burner and start exploring possible areas of co-operation. Under Gorbachev, there was a strong Soviet desire to normalise the relation with China and get out of conflict situations in Afghanistan as well as Kampuchea. Gorbachev's steps eventually led to the end of the cold war. In this region there was suspicion about India's naval activities which necessitated clarification and building of mutual confidence. The Naval intentions of India had been distorted by media and vested interest in this region. There was also the introduction of one window clearance to reduce bureaucratic hurdle for investment purposes. Its purpose was to encourage meaningful economic engagement with economically vibrant extended eastern neighbours. The political exchanges between India and the Southeast Asia during Rajiv Gandhi's period focused on the search for energy co-operation in the field of science and technology, avoiding of double taxation. The FICCI took the lead of business delegation in visiting ASEAN countries.

LEP of India is not merely an external economic policy but is a strategic shift in India's vision of the world and India's place in the evolving global economy. India is so situated that she is the pivot of southern and South-East-Asia. In the past our culture flowed to all these countries and they came to us in many ways. Most South East Asian countries have long standing cultural and religious ties which have survived the onslaught of time. India's new and revamped approach towards the region east of India was dubbed as the 'Look East' Policy. This was the brainchild of the then Prime Minister Narasimha Rao. Under the leadership of Narashima Rao and Manmohan Singh the relation between India and Southeast Asia blossomed. Most of these countries of Southeast Asia view India as upholding a strong democratic ethos and a benign foreign policy of mutual co-existence based on the ideas of Gandhi and Nehru. As consequences, India has benefited from the Look East Policy as it has boosted defence cooperation with Myanmar, Indonesia, Vietnam and Thailand. (Goswami, 2009) As discussed earlier Look East Policy turned out to be of strategic importance for both India and SEA during the period of globalisation.

Globalisation and Look East Policy

Trade and investment along with financial surges are the benefits of globalisation. In fact, trade and investment are more and more complementary and indivisible in the process of globalisation. India has also been impacted by globalisation. The end of cold war and growing significance of geo-economic factors led to fundamental reorientation in India's foreign policy. The paradigmatic shift led to the adoption of liberalisation, privatisation, and globalisation (LPG) programmes in domestic sphere subsequently leading to formation of a framework of India's LEP. (Yadav, 2011) This Policy coincided with the liberalisation of its economy in 1991. But at present India's north-east region has a vital role in India's Look East Policy. India needs north-eastern region in its Look East Policy for better connectivity with Southeast Asia by land route.

Indian market has experienced substantial change in the last few decades especially since it took to open market policy way back in 1990's. As a result India's integration with world economy is in progress at a significant rate. Most of the major powers of the world have their eye on the emerging market of India. The immediate neighbours in South East Asia therefore need to be familiar with the reality and should formulate strategy to enter into the trade link. India's search for a new type of economic relation with Southeast Asia is not only prompted by consideration of globalisation but by the desire to seek the development of the NE by increasing its connectivity with the outside world. Due to globalisation some countries of South East Asia like Thailand, Indonesia, Malaysia and Singapore and East Asia like Taiwan, Hongkong, South Korea got economic prosperity. Hence it is natural that India would be tempted to establish trade relation with these countries. Look East Policy tried to attach importance to SEA and its regional organisation ASEAN. In the initial phase, it was driven mainly by forces of energy and economic requirements. Later on political and strategic dimension were taken into consideration. Before we discussed about ASEAN and Look East Policy and its role with India, it should be clear about SEA and the ASEAN.

South East Asian Nations and Formation of ASEAN

Southeast Asia consists of the countries that are geographically South of India to the East of China. It comprises 11 nations, namely Brunei, Cambodia, East Timor, Indonesia, Laos, Malaysia, Myanmar (or Burma), Philippines, Singapore, Thailand and Vietnam. Moreover, the region Southeast Asia can be divided into two sub-regions. First, mainland Southeast Asia includes

Cambodia, Laos, Malaysia, Myanmar, Thailand and Vietnam. Second, island Southeast Asia comprises Brunei, East Timor, Indonesia, Singapore, Philippines, and parts of Malaysia i.e. east Malaysia. All of the nations are members of the ASEAN, expect East Timor. It is an observer state. Trade relation or economic cooperation among Southeast Asian states has a long custom. The impact of colonial rule, struggle for independence and in some cases war influenced the economic attitudes and policies of those SEA nations. The purpose of formation of ASEAN is to accelerate the economic growth, social progress and cultural development in the region through joint endeavours in the spirit of equality and partnership in order to strengthen the foundation for a prosperous and peaceful community of SEA nations. ASEAN provides a forum for the integration of commerce, and regional responses to international concerns. Though geographically Indonesia is the largest country in Southeast Asian region, all the major five South East Asian nations; Singapore, Malaysia, Indonesia, the Philippines and Thailand have socio-economic importance and cultural legacy of their own. If we take ASEAN as a single unit, it would rank as the sixth largest economy in the world, behind USA, China, Japan, India and Germany.

Gate Way

In contemporary era, physical connectivity is of utmost importance as it channelises the means to accelerate the movement of goods, people and services and thereby acts as a gateway to reviving economic enterprise. In his speech Prime Minister Manmohan Singh referred to India's north-east as a gateway to 'Asian Century'. Recognizing the advent of globalisation, regional economic cooperation, new policy approaches for development and the massive changes taking place in the domestic and external fronts, and Northeast India has enormous potential to exploit by taking 'geography as opportunity'. He stated that 'with the paradigm shift from state centrism to interdependence and global and regional cooperation, India is aware of the geo-economic potential of the North-Eastern region as a gateway to East and South-East Asia.' The economic potentials of this policy emphasize a link to the economic interests of the North-eastern region as a whole. Northeast India as the gateway to the East and Southeast Asia and it is one major initiative undertaken by the government of India in the present times. The proposed development of the North-eastern region is to be brought in through increased trade and investment and engaging the people of the region in productive and profitable activities to end their alienation. The Look East Policy by addressing the peculiarity of the area and the problems involved with it can bring lasting peace and development in the region. (Haokip, 2012)

Bilateral projects of India and South East Asia with special focus to North East India

India has initiated some bilateral projects and also become party to some multilateral projects, aimed at enhancing connectivity between the Northeast and Southeast Asia. The Look East Policy is expected to usher in a new era of development for the Northeast through roads, railway lines, river transport, network of pipelines, air connectivity, tourism infrastructure, border check-posts, educational, and health infrastructure, etc. for development. Though in SEA there was a time when India use to be looked at with suspicion because of its proximity to Soviet Union and some SEA powers were opposed to the expansion of the then Soviet Russia influence. But now this doesn't hold good and this has resulted in tremendous growth in trade relation of India with SEA. Most of the intellectual respondents are at one with the view that there has been a paradigmatic shift from the cold war period to present phase of globalisation so far as the LEP is concerned. Moreover, India's Northeast region will be repositioned as a regional trading hub. It is evident that the Trilateral Highway is crucial for the realisation of the LEP and its failure might shake the very foundations of this quest upon which India has embarked. However, in the mid-2000s some transportation experts were skeptical about the viability of the project given the economic and political climate in both South and South-East Asia. Several measures have been undertaken under the aegis of the Look East Policy to uplift North East India such as the "Asian Highway",

"Asian Railway link" and "Natural Gas pipeline". Moreh -Tamu—Kalewa Road, Kaladan Multimodal project, India-Myanmar-Thailand Trilateral Highway/Trans Asian Highway, India-Myanmar rail linkages, the Stilwell road, Myanmar-India-Bangladesh gas and oil pipeline, Tamanthi Hydroelectricity project and optical fiber network between Northeast India and Southeast Asia.

- The 160-km long India–Myanmar Friendship Road linking Tamu-Kalemyo-Kalewa was built on 2001. In August 2017, the government of India allocated US$256 million for the upgrade of 1,360 kilometres (850 mi) highway from Moreh in Manipur through Tamu, Myanmar to Mae Sot in Thailand. On 6 September 2017, the National Highway Authority of India awarded a 1,200 crore (US$180 million) construction and maintenance road contract for the Kalewa-Yagyi section in Myanmar to a joint venture of Punj Lloyd and Varaha Infra Ltd. The 120 km stretch will be upgraded to a two-lane road. The engineering, procurement and construction contract for the project will entirely be funded by the Indian Foreign Ministry.
- To develop connectivity through water, ASEAN and India are working on the Kaladan Multi-Modal Transit Transport Project (KMMTTP). The project was initiated by the Indian government in 2008 and is entirely funded by India. The purpose is to seek an alternative route through Myanmar for the transportation of goods to the northeast region of India. The Kaladan Multi-modal Transit Transport facility is aimed at establishing connectivity between Indian ports and Sittwe port in Myanmar through riverine transport and road links in Mizoram. This will provide an alternative route for transport of goods to Northeast India.
- A road is also planned to connect Paletwa in Myanmar to Zorinpui on the India-Myanmar border. Alongside this initiative, India has contributed to build a sea link via Sittwe port in Myanmar in order to enable an alternative transit route through Bangladesh.

- With the Ganga Mekong initiative there is potential for direct flights between Guwahati-Ho-Chi Minh cities – Imphal – Hanoi. Improvement is needed in railway connectivity to neighbouring countries and developments of air circuits between North-East Region are important. Guwahati needs to be projected as an IT gateway to South East Asia.

ASEAN-India Car Rally

- The then Indian prime minister Atal Bihari Vajpayee proposed 1st ASEAN-India Car Rally was held from 23 November - 6 December 2004, which involved about 240 participants with 60 vehicles. Then, the journey started in Guwahati, India, and traversed to Myanmar, Thailand, the Lao PDR, Viet Nam, Cambodia, Malaysia and Singapore before ending in Batam, Indonesia. This is the 2nd edition of the ASEAN-India Car Rally has been concluded 21 December 2012. The rally began in Yogyakarta Indonesia, with a ceremonial flag-off in Singapore and wind its way through 8 of the 10 ASEAN countries before finally ending in New Delhi, India. The Rally kicked off on 26 November 2012 in Yogyakarta, Indonesia, with a Ceremonial Flag-Off in Singapore and wound its way through 8 of the 10 ASEAN Member States. On 17 December 2012, the journey finished in Guwahati, India, before it was officially concluded today by the Heads of State/Government of ASEAN and India here in New Delhi. 31 Mahindra XUV 500 took part in this rally covering about 8000 km through 8 Asian countries. This measure clearly reflects the existence of land route connectivity that could facilitate free flow of trade, investment and tourism between ASEAN and India. As one of the most highlighted events in commemorating the 20th Anniversary of the ASEAN-India Dialogue Relations in 2012, the Rally's main objective is to essentially demonstrate, in a very visible manner, India's proximity to ASEAN, which will also enhance public awareness of the current canvas of ASEAN-India partnership and further strengthen trade, investment, tourism and people-to-people linkages.

- **Trans-Asian Railway**

  Moreh is a town located on the India-Myanmar border. It has huge commercial hub, and economists suggested that it could become a bustling city in the next couple of decades. The town is already seen as the commercial capital of Manipur and India's Gateway to South-East Asia. Manipur stated that the North East Region was closely interlinked with Myanmar and Bangladesh. The opening of border trade in Moreh had somewhat helped to restore bilateral trade between Manipur and Myanmar. It had good agro climate, fertile land yields orchids and medicinal plants for export which has been discussed in second chapter. But some improvement will be needed for transport facility. Airport at Imphal could become a potential air link between North East India and South Asia. A flight from Imphal (Manipur) and Chiangmai (Thailand) would take only one hour. As of 2012, all freight traffic from Asia to Europe goes by sea. The Trans-Asian Railway will enable containers from Singapore, China, Vietnam, Cambodia, India, Bangladesh, Myanmar, Thailand and Korea to travel over land by train to Europe. The Southern Corridor of the Trans-Asian Railway (TAR) is of prime interest to India. It connects Yunnan in China and Thailand with Europe via Turkey and passes through India. There is a general understanding between India and Myanmar that their railways will be interconnected via a 346-km line section that will extend from Kalay in Myanmar to Jiribam in India via the border point at Tamu/Moreh, India.

Tourism and Banking Sector

The Shukla Committee, which was constituted in 1998, came out with its recommendations for the promotion of the tourism and banking sectors in NER. The committee emphasized the need for an international airport in Guwahati. It suggested to attract foreign tourism through special international packages in consultation with neighbouring countries like Bangladesh, Bhutan, Nepal, Myanmar and Thailand.

Regarding banking sector development in the north-east, the committee recommended improving the credit-deposit (CD) ratio and to considering industrial finance as a part of priority sector lending. The Committee suggested cross subsidisation of the interest rates and reintroduction of capital investment subsidy in the region. The government, RBI and all-India financial institutes should provide adequate funds to enable the newly established North Eastern Development Financial Corporation to perform its role effectively in the region. The State Governments should put maximum effort to create an investor friendly environment to attract more private capital.(Northeast Region Vision 2020)

Manipur is a strategic point to connect the North East with Southeast Asian markets. Moreover improved connectivity of the northeastern states can end the region's geopolitical isolation, boost social and economic mobility and market integration. "The Government of India's approach to the development of the Northeast is an urgent and speedy enhancement of connectivity. This is a multi-modal programme, across land, water and air," Manipur is a strategic point to connect the North East with Southeast Asian markets. Moreover improved connectivity of the northeastern states can end the region's geopolitical isolation, boost social and economic mobility and market integration. "The Government of India's approach to the development of the Northeast is an urgent and speedy enhancement of connectivity. This is a multi-modal programme, across land, water and air," the present president Ramnath Kovind said in the north-east development summit on 2017 November.

Air Connectivity

- To increase Regional Air connectivity with mainland of the country Imphal will get a direct flight service to New Delhi from the first day of the coming year. Union civil aviation minister Jayant Sinha, making the announcement at the Summit said the flight will be operated by Air India twice a week and it would gradually be converted into a daily service. Manipur Governor Najma Heptulla further urged for direct flights services to other major cities like Chennai, Bangaluru and Mumbai as well.

- 19 "new airports or underserved airports", including More in Manipur, Rupsi in Assam, and Tura in Meghalaya will be added to the country's civil aviation network. Further 17 new heliports will be opened in the region.
- International flights connecting Guwahati with Dhaka (Bangladesh), Kathmandu (Nepal), Yangon (Myanmar), Yunnan (China) and Bangkok (Thailand). Manipur, Arunachal Pradesh, Nagaland and Mizoram share boundaries with Myanmar, India's gateway to the ASEAN nations, but there is no direct flight from any of the northeastern states and people in this region have to go via Kolkata to reach Myanmar. Among the ten states of ASEAN, Myanmar is the only nation that India shares both a land and maritime border with.

Inland Waterways

Inland waterways bid a prospect for strengthening the local economy and connecting one of India's most isolated northeast regions to the wider region.

- Utilisations and operationalisations of Inland Waterways through riverine routes between North East India
- The Multi-modal Kaladan River Project
- Construction of Sittwe Sea Port Project in Myanmar as earliest.

Technology Mission

The Centrally Sponsored TMNE scheme is operational since 2001-02 in the 8 NE states of Arunachal Pradesh, Assam, Manipur, Meghalaya, Mizoram, Nagaland, Tripura and Sikkim. During Tenth

Plan (2003-04), the scheme has been extended to other 03 Himalayan states of J&K, Himachal Pradesh and Uttarakhand, in addition to North Eastern states making the TMNE operational in 11 states. The TMNE comprises of four Mini missions viz. MM-I (Research), MM-II (Production and Productivity), MM-III (PHM and Marketing) and MM-IV (Processing). The scheme gets 100% financial assistance from the centre. The TMNE envisages to harness the potential of Horticulture, maximize economic, ecological and social benefits through desirable diversification, develop infrastructure for production of planting material, storage and processing and to generate gainfull employment. The outlay during Ninth and Tenth Plan was Rs 229.38 crores and Rs 845.00 crores (NE states – Rs 585.00 crores + Himalayan States - Rs 260.00 crores), respectively. The Eleventh Plan has an outlay of Rs 1500.00 crores. Against an outlay of Rs 323.40 crores, during 2007-08, the reported expenditure was Rs 321.76 crores. The outlay (RE) for 2008-09 was Rs 384.00 crores with the reported expenditure of Rs 291.39 crores. During the year 2009-10 the allocation for the scheme is Rs 349.00 crores (Rs 280.00 crores for NE States + Rs 69.00 crores for Himalayan states. Till 2008-09, an additional 4.94 lac hectares were brought under horticulture cultivation (i.e. fruits - > 3 lac hectares , vegetables - 0.78 lac hectares and spices- 0.62 lac hectares) including plantation crops, medicinal/Aromatic plants and flowers etc. Further, 47 wholesale markets; 262 rural primary markets; 64 Apni mandies; 18 State Grading Laboratories; 31 Ropeways and 49 processing units have been established in addition to 935 model nurseries, 10,032 Community tanks, 11,106 Tubewells, 26 tissue culture units, 25 model Floriculture centers, 25 mushroom units and about 25 lac sq. meter of Green Houses have been created.

The existing possibilities in the process of enhancing connectivity between India's Northeast and Southeast Asia is not a cakewalk because there are also geographical, technical, political and security challenges that limit the process of infrastructure development. (Yogendra Singh, 2008)

Trilateral Highway

- The completion of the Trilateral Highway will forge greater connectivity between India and Southeast Asia and the positives will outweigh the negatives in every sense. Connectivity will bring its share of problems but will certainly open up avenues for cooperation with the neighbouring states and provide effective mechanisms for dealing with cross-border problems which hitherto have remained unresolved. Additionally, the Trilateral Highway will connect India to the Asian Highway Network and trade between India and ASEAN will receive a further boost. The India–Myanmar–Thailand Trilateral Highway is a highway under construction under India's Look East Policy that will connect Moreh, India with Mae Sot, Thailand via Myanmar. Imphal-Mandalay-Bangkok 1,980 km (1,230 mi) route, consisting of Imphal-Mandalay 584 km (363 mi) and Mandalay-Bangkok 1,397 km (868 mi), is good condition highway except for the under upgrade 101 km (63 mi) part of 120 km (75 mi) long Kalewa-Yagyi stretch, revised expected completion date for which is 2019.The road is expected to boost trade and commerce in the ASEAN–India Free Trade Area, as well as with the rest of Southeast Asia. India has also proposed extending the highway to Cambodia, Laos and Vietnam. India and ASEAN have plans to extend this route to Laos, Cambodia and Vietnam as this connectivity will generate annually, an estimated US$70 billion in incremental GDP and 20 million in incremental aggregate employment by 2025, and India has offered US$1 billion line-of-credit for the India-ASEAN connectivity projects. Thus, the trade transaction of India with SEA was increased manifold which is focused in Table 2.1.

Prospects of Regional Organisation

The long term objective has been to establish its supremacy in Asia by countering the lengthening shadow of the United States, in East Asia, and to curb the influence of India, the other rising Asian power and a perceived rival, in South Asia, India's traditional backyard, and also in Southeast Asia, which India has rediscovered with its Look East Policy. Super power like USA, China desires to maintain dominance over the regional grouping. With legitimate trade and transit interests, trans crossing the South China Sea, the role of the external stakeholders has been very much welcome. Robust political, economic and even defence cooperation with all the important actors is an essential prerequisite for attaining such an objective. Indonesia's membership of the G-20 has also strengthened its role in the ASEAN. This has undoubtedly granted Indonesia a greater say in ASEAN affairs, particularly in its stated objective of democratizing the ASEAN charter. Indonesia's offer at the ASEAN summit in Hua Hin, Thailand in October 2009 to "coordinate" with the other member states before future G-20 summits allayed the fears of other members of the organisation of being neglected by their largest and influential member and has given it the status of ASEAN's international spokesman. The super powers want to keep up their sphere of influence on the regional framework. The benign neglect of Southeast Asia in the post-Cold War period by the United States together with the growing military and economic might of China has tilted the current regional power balance in favour of the latter. This is obviously a matter of major concern for both India and the countries of ASEAN, as their interests converge in ensuring that the region is not dominated by any single power. The US, Japan, India and to an extent Australia have often taken on the offshore balancing role in the region. However, it is worth noting that regional organisation can better grow if there is no dictation by the outside powers.

India and ASEAN

India's interest to strengthen multi-faceted relationship with ASEAN is a consequence of the major changes in the world's political and economic scenario since the early 1990s. India and ASEAN are natural partners due to geographical proximity and tradition of cultural interaction. However, the economic crisis of 1991 along with the collapse of the Soviet Union, India's only economic and strategic partner, the end of the Cold War and the onset of globalisation made India realise that the best means for development would come through promotion of international trade and attracting foreign investments. India's own march towards economic liberalisation is search for economic space resulted in the 'Look East Policy', which is an economic policy of engagement with Southeast Asia as an official initiative in achieving two objectives: the encouragement of trade links with individual partners and to provide foreign employment for India's own expanding work force. India's relations with South East Asia/ ASEAN can be characterised as having passed through three phrase i.e. Dialogue Partnership, Summit Level Partnership, and Strategic Partnership (Beuria, 2018) India's interaction has started as a sectoral dialogue partner of ASEAN in 1992 on areas such as trade, investment, tourism and science and technology. Mutual interest for a wider engagement was the main interest of India and ASEAN. India was invited as a full dialogue partner of ASEAN during the Fifth ASEAN Summit in Bangkok in December 1995. The implication of India for Asia's regional security prompted ASEAN also to invite India to be a member of the ASEAN Regional Forum (ARF) in July 1996. However, the most important milestone was achieved with the hosting of the first ASEAN India summit in Phnom Penh, Cambodia during November 2002, which came as a result of strong signals of economic co-operation from India provided by a series of bilateral visits by Indian leaders to existing as well as smaller and newer members of ASEAN.

Performance of India's trade with ASEAN in comparison with world trade during 2001-16

During the period of Modi's foreign policy, neighbourhood got added priority and a renewed desire to make India emerge a global power got a concrete shape. This found expression in pursuing a vigorous trade policy with different regional organisations including ASEAN.(Mohanty et.al, 2017) Co-operation between ASEAN and India is expected to encompass a strategic and political partnership, thus going well beyond a traditional Free Trade Agreement (FTA).

The following Table 2.1 is basically focused on India and ASEAN trade relations expressed in terms of exports and imports during 2001-1016. This is analyzed in terms of percentage of India's exports to and import from ASEAN in proportion to its total exports to and imports from the world. Table 2.1 reflects India's exports to and imports from the world as well as to ASEAN and the exports to and imports from ASEAN as a proportion of total exports to and imports from the world, expressed in terms of percentage.

Table 2.1: India's Export to and Import from ASEAN in comparison with world trade

Unit-Thousand USD

India's	Export To ASEAN			India's	Import ASEAN	From	Trade Balance
Year	World	ASEAN	%	World	ASEAN	%	
2001	43878489	3315112	7.6	50671106	4345489	8.6	2726966
2002	50097958	4503303	9.0	57453469	4807277	8.4	2508544
2003	59360659	5071800	8.5	72430524	6686881	9.2	4045337
2004	75904200	7552218	9.9	98981129	8549995	8.6	3858889
2005	100352637	10285769	10.2	140861667	10632023	7.5	6529817
2006	121200606	12369341	10.2	178212440	16300608	9.1	8610758
2007	145898053	13824081	9.5	218645294	21031035	9.6	11440221
2008	181860898	19433467	10.7	315712106	26698438	8.5	11554719
2009	176765036	17898835	10.1	266401553	23968100	9.0	12905730
2010	220408496	22958453	10.4	350029387	29640182	8.5	17171964
2011	301483250	34497614	11.4	462402791	40331863	8.7	17641513
2012	289564769	32295000	11.2	488976378	42737956	8.7	15240679
2013	336611389	37885468	11.3	466045567	42308784	9.1	16254131
2014	317544642	31294246	9.9	459369464	44457579	9.7	19370039
2015	264381004	26428121	10.0	390744731	41516394	10.6	20258259
2016	260326912	26381170	10.1	356704792	38222455	10.7	13757880
CAGR	14.71%	16.39%		16.38%	17.74%		

Source: http://www.trademap.org/stdatasources.

India's exports to the ASEAN in proportion to the world exports has increased from 7.6% in 2001 to 11.4% in 2011 and it has declined in recent years to 10.1% in 2016, whereas India's imports from ASEAN in proportion to India's total imports from the world have increased from 8.6% in 2001 to 10.7% in 2016.The compound annual growth rate of exports to and imports from ASEAN have increased at 16.39% and 17.74% respectively and which is more than that of the trade relation with the world. The figures of trade balance indicate India is having favourable trade balance with

ASEAN. The size of the positive trade balance has increased over the study period with some fluctuations. The trend of exports and imports between India and ASEAN countries reflects increasing trade openness in the last fifteen years.

In 2001, India's export to ASEAN was 7.6% and at the same time India's import from ASEAN was 8.6%. But since 2002 the India's export to ASEAN was 9.0% of exports to total world which was higher compared to imports. India's export to ASEAN touched the highest value ever during 2011-13 i.e. 11.4%. After that till 2016 it was little bit on decline and touched 10.1% in 2016. It is to be noted that ASEAN is India's fourth largest trading partner. India became the third dialogue partner of ASEAN to set off an ASEAN Connectivity Coordinating Committee-India Meeting. While India has made extensive progress in implementing the India-Myanmar-Thailand Trilateral Highway and the Kaladan Multimodal Project, issues related to increasing the maritime and air connectivity between ASEAN and India. One important thing is that export percentage is higher than import during the years 2002, 2004, 2005, and 2006, 2008-2014. In 2015 and 2016 India's Import from ASEAN has increased in comparison with India's export to ASEAN. (Mohanty, *et.al,* 2017)

India's export to and Import from 10 ASEAN Nations

History must reveal that the ASEAN's engagement with India has seen some important milestones for deepening economic and political relations ever since the end of the Cold War and India's determined pursuit of a Look East Policy since 1991, which has already been focused previously. ASEAN India trade picked up momentum in the nineties barring the East Asian crisis period. Recent years witnessed the growth of trade between them at double digit rate. The inherent potential of this trade is revealed in rising India's exports to the region and the necessity felt to investigate the gains achieved in the process of building of the economic relations between the two. India-ASEAN engagements at the summit level and all the ensuing developments have helped India to become a credible interlocutor with the major powers of the world. Singapore is the one which inked maximum number of regional agreements, where India, Singapore and Thailand are involved in maximum number of regional agreements in Asia. India's reciprocity in 1994 is marked through the joint anti-submarine warfare exercises. A two pronged strategy adopted by Singapore and India has intensified their relations. Singapore and India conducted first (SINDEX 04) and second bilateral air exercises at Gwalior in 2004 and Kalaikunda near Kolkata in January 2006 respectively. In 2004, Singapore was granted training facilities for its army and air force on Indian soil. This marked an unprecedented step for India which usually avoided foreign military presence of any type on its territory. Joint naval exercise with Singapore was also undertaken in South China Sea in 2005.The Indian defence production network is all set to cater to the needs of Malaysia for its defence modernisation programme, Malaysia also sought help of India in the training of the Sukhoi pilots and industrial cooperation of Hindustan Aeronautics Limited. (Jha, 2011) The commitment and efforts by India to intensify its economic relations with ASEAN are evident from a Framework Agreement on Comprehensive Economic Co-operation between ASEAN and India in October 2003, being signed by the Indian Prime Minister during the Second ASEAN-India Summit in Bali. Table 2.2 outlines the share of individual member countries of ASEAN in India's Exports to ASEAN for the period under study. As earlier, It has been made clear that all South East Asian nations are members of ASEAN except one nation i.e. Timor.

With economic liberalisation among ASEAN members Malaysia, Thailand and Singapore became the major source of FDI in to India. From negligible amount in 1991, cumulative approved FDI from ASEAN reached more than $5 Billion. (Chakraborti, 2009) Indian Bureaucrats, allegedly had wanted to delay signing an FTA (Free Trade Agreement) on goods until ASEAN members had agreed to conclude an FTA on services and investment but they were overruled by Prime Minister Manmohan Singh who was trying to use the FTA to send a political and not just economic signal to the region. However, India ASEAN FTA on goods adopted in August 2009 in the teeth of critical domestic opposition from farmers in India is perhaps the most striking evidence of the strategic priority attached by New delhi to

Table 2.2: India's export to ten ASEAN Nations and the growth rate during 2001-16

Year	ASEAN	Singapore	Vietnam	Malaysia	Indonesia	Thailand	Philippines	Myanmar	Cambodia	Brunei Darussalam	Laos
		%	%	%	%	%	%	%	%	%	%
2001	3315112	27.93	6.57	23.77	14.38	18.05	6.99	1.74	0.32	0.07	0.17
2002	4503303	30.65	6.76	16.49	17.09	16.46	10.38	1.64	0.38	0.10	0.04
2003	5071800	33.56	7.47	15.64	20.50	14.43	6.39	1.51	0.40	0.10	0.01
2004	7552218	45.24	7.08	13.77	15.96	11.35	4.81	1.49	0.22	0.07	0.01
2005	10285769	52.77	6.16	11.12	13.51	10.30	4.69	1.14	0.21	0.04	0.06
2006	12369341	49.54	7.07	10.76	15.12	10.92	4.83	1.00	0.39	0.36	0.02
2007	13824081	46.22	8.98	13.38	13.59	12.10	4.13	1.18	0.32	0.06	0.02
2008	19433467	45.56	9.33	15.61	13.68	10.32	3.89	1.22	0.28	0.09	0.02
2009	17898835	38.15	10.24	19.69	16.78	9.56	3.90	1.16	0.23	0.14	0.15
2010	22958453	39.49	10.78	15.49	19.85	9.32	3.49	1.19	0.27	0.09	0.04
2011	34497614	45.30	10.05	11.01	18.55	8.02	2.92	1.32	0.26	2.52	0.04
2012	32295000	41.97	11.33	11.74	18.65	10.70	3.47	1.63	0.34	0.10	0.08
2013	37885468	37.45	15.80	14.51	14.67	11.10	3.88	1.96	0.36	0.11	0.16
2014	31294246	30.92	20.86	14.83	14.20	10.99	4.59	2.78	0.49	0.14	0.20
2015	26428121	29.53	20.27	18.51	10.86	11.78	4.94	3.25	0.55	0.11	0.19
2016	26381170	27.88	22.58	15.88	11.87	11.23	5.59	4.33	0.41	0.14	0.09
CAGR	**16.39**	**15.4**	**26.75**	**15.79**	**14.87**	**13.55**	**12.4**	**22.64**	**19.2**	**23.15**	**29.82**

Source: http://www.trademap.org/stDataSources

commercial relations with the region. It is interesting to note that in 2009 only 2.5% of ASEAN's trade was with India in comparison to 11.6% with China. But in the three years since the FTA was signed trade with ASEAN has grown up by 30%. (Tharoor, 2012). This will be further proved when data regarding trade relation between India and the individual member countries of ASEAN are presented subsequently.

The following table (Table 2.2) focused on India's exports with 10 Individual nations of South East Asia. It needs to be emphasized that among all ASEAN member countries five nations are the top export destination. Those states are Singapore, Viet Nam, Malaysia, Indonesia, and Thailand. India's export to ASEAN touched the highest value ever during 2013 i.e. 37885468 thousand USD.

Singapore stood as first export destination of India in comparison to other SEA nations. The second was Indonesia during 2001-2012. From 2013 onward Vietnam secured the second position. India's export is very low to Brunei and Laos in the context of relative percentage but Compound Annual Growth rate is high at 23.15% and 29.82% respectively. Trend and growth of India's exports to various ASEAN nations during the period from 2001-16 shows that Singapore is the nation with whom India has the highest percentage of exports of total exports to ASEAN countries, followed by Malaysia, Thailand and Indonesia respectively, countries of ASEAN such as Vietnam, Brunei, Myanmar and Cambodia though had a lesser share of total exports from India to ASEAN, have experienced a higher growth rate in terms of value of exports compared to other member countries during the study period. The compound growth rate of total exports to Vietnam, Brunei, Myanmar and Cambodia are 26.75%, 23.15%, 22.64% and 19.2% percent respectively which are more than the compound growth of total exports to ASEAN countries.

It is worth probing whether this scenario is the result of the emergence of CLMV (Cambodia, Laos PDR, Myanmar, and Vietnam). It is observed that the growth of India's Exports to Cambodia, Laos, Brunei and Myanmar, Vietnam also confirm that ASEAN on the whole has great trade potential and Indo-ASEAN trade has a lot of scope for future. The growth rate of Vietnam also

Table 2.3: India's Import from Ten ASEAN nations and the growth rate during 2001-16

YEAR	ASEAN	Indonesia	Malaysia	Singapore	Thailand	Vietnam	Philippines	Myanmar	Cambodia	Brunei Darussalam	Laos
		%	%	%	%	%	%	%	%	%	
2001	4345489	22.25	26.52	31.18	9.77	0.40	1.79	8.06	0.03	0.01	0
2002	4807277	26.28	27.68	27.74	7.59	0.58	2.76	7.34	0.01	0.01	667
2003	6686881	28.11	28.33	27.92	8.06	0.50	1.67	5.39	0.00	0.01	209
2004	8549995	28.39	25.90	29.15	8.77	0.86	2.12	4.80	0.00	0.01	92
2005	10632023	28.39	22.91	29.72	11.25	1.20	1.91	4.60	0.00	0.01	72
2006	16300608	22.15	28.56	31.81	9.51	0.98	1.28	4.31	0.01	1.38	376
2007	21031035	23.02	27.22	32.82	10.42	0.73	0.83	3.85	0.01	1.11	80
2008	26698438	24.09	27.95	31.11	9.98	1.39	0.85	3.39	0.02	1.22	525
2009	23968100	31.71	20.82	25.62	11.58	1.85	1.43	4.93	0.02	2.04	194
2010	29640182	32.71	20.23	24.50	13.30	3.35	1.33	3.79	0.03	0.70	0.07
2011	40331863	34.62	22.58	20.22	12.53	3.85	1.12	3.13	0.02	1.75	0.17
2012	42737956	39.92	24.55	18.24	12.87	4.55	1.16	3.15	0.02	2.20	0.34
2013	42308784	35.42	22.05	16.61	12.94	6.68	0.97	3.23	0.03	1.81	0.26
2014	44457579	34.16	24.58	15.90	12.78	6.26	0.90	3.13	0.04	2.12	0.13
2015	41516394	33.49	23.03	17.81	13.61	6.46	1.25	2.45	0.10	1.46	0.34
2016	38222455	31.89	22.64	17.58	13.91	8.13	1.24	2.84	0.11	1.21	0.45
CAGR	34.56%	20.77	16.08	12.27	22.08	45.45	12.35	10.46	39.16	84.76	

Source: http://www.trademap.org/stdatasources

proves this New Delhi's views on Vietnam as "a strong pillar" of its AEP, whereas Vietnam supports the policy, but wants India to play a more active role in the region's affairs. (Vinh, 2016)

The Table 2.3 focused on India's import from ten Individual states of SEA. Among those ten country India's import is maximum from five nations those are Singapore, Malaysia, Thailand, Indonesia and Vietnam. Among these five countries Singapore, Malaysia and Indonesia has good import value with some fluctuation in some years. But India's import from Vietnam and Thailand is impressively increasing import value at present. Here we may say that the relationship is maintaining in a positive way. Especially India's import from Vietnam is very positive sign and there is no fluctuation during the study period. The Table 2.2 and 2.3 has made a critical analysis with India and South East Asian nations during 2001-16.

SINGAPORE

From the Table 2.2 and 2.3 it can noted that Singapore was one of the first to respond to India's "Look East" Policy of expanding its economic, cultural and strategic ties in Southeast Asia to strengthen its standing as a regional power. India and Singapore share long-standing cultural, commercial and strategic relations, with Singapore being a part of the "Greater India" cultural and commercial region. India's economic liberalisation and its "Look East" Policy have led to a major expansion in bilateral trade. India's export to Singapore has grew from 27.93% in 2001 to 52.77% in 2005 and with little decrease 45.30% in 2011. India's main exports to Singapore in 2005 included petroleum, gemstones, jewellery, machinery and its imports from Singapore included electronic goods, organic chemicals and metals. More than half of Singapore's exports to India are basically "re-exports" – items that had been imported from India. Singapore has also engaged in joint naval exercises with India, including anti-submarine warfare, search and rescue operations, and in conducting joint anti-piracy exercises near and around the Straits of Malacca and the Bay of Bengal. The joint patrolling of the seas by the two nations have been extremely helpful in protecting the commercial sea lanes, cutting off drug trafficking, curbing arms smuggling and preventing maritime terrorism. (Alam, 2011) The Singapore India Maritime Bilateral Exercise 2017 (SIMBEX-17) has concluded. Apart from SIMBEX, the two navies also interact regularly through professional exchange programmes, staff talks and training courses. On 29 November 2017, the two countries signed a naval cooperation agreement aimed at boosting maritime security, joint exercises and mutual logistics support. The agreement also permits ships of either navy to refuel, restock and, rearm at each other military bases.

VIETNAM

The Government of India had formulated the Look East Policy with the vision that the whole North East of India and South Asian economies are similar in nature and such a strategic policy would be mutually acceptable and beneficial to one another giving ample opportunities for cooperation and integration. India is the 13th-largest exporter to Vietnam, with exports has grown steadily from 6.57% in 2001 to 22.58% by 2016.Vietnam's exports to India rose to 0.40% 2001 to 8.13% 2016. India and Vietnam have also expanded cooperation in information technology, education and collaboration of the respective national space programmes. Direct air links and lax visa regulations have been established to bolster tourism. Thus, India should give MFN (Most Favoured Nation) status to Vietnam since both statuses always give high importance to each other in terms of trade, commerce and economic cooperation. India is providing training support for Vietnam's Kilo-class submarines. India has also offered to train Vietnamese pilots to fly Sukhoi aircraft. India is providing a $100 million credit line to Vietnam that allows Vietnam to buy defence equipment from India. During his visit to Vietnam, on 02 September 2016, India's Prime Minister Narendra Modi announced a new line of credit US$500 million for procurement of defence equipment. India is selling Vietnam four large patrol vessels that will enable Vietnam to patrol its waters and Vietnam is also interested in buying BrahMos short range cruise missiles.

INDONESIA

India views Indonesia, the largest country in Southeast Asia, as a strategic partner that can play an important role in its Look East Policy. Indonesia is not only the most populous country in the region but also has the largest Muslim population in the world. Both India and Indonesia are facing rising threats from Islamic militancy and terrorism arising from the changing nature of Islam. Indonesia has done well in fighting terrorism. Most Indonesians practice a synergetic, moderate form of Islam. Yet a small band of home grown extremists is waging a bloody jihad. The growing popularity of Islam makes it all the more imperative for India to help Indonesia in its democratisation process, for pluralism and democracy can be major bulwarks against militancy and exclusive Islam. Indonesia is the country that literally connects the Indian Ocean region with the Pacific region. Prime Minister Narendra Modi's proposed visit to Indonesia this year will lift the partnership to the next level. What is imperative at this stage is to promote people-to-people ties between India and Indonesia, incidentally a country that has taken its name and derived the name of its currency from India, and named its airlines Garuda after Vishnu's mount. (Roy, 2018) Both countries maintain extradition and Mutual Legal Assistance treaties aimed at strengthening cooperation in combating transnational crime and terrorism. India and Indonesia conducted a 17-day joint coordinated patrol exercise in the Andaman Sea in October. This was the 28th such coordinated patrol and second bilateral maritime exercise between both countries. Both countries have also established several bilateral agreements and exchanges aimed at strengthening strategic cooperation. This includes Foreign Office consultations since 2013, the Joint Defence Cooperation Committee set up in 2007, a New Strategic Partnership in 2005, a Memorandum of Understanding on combating terrorism in 2004, the India-Indonesia Joint Commission co-chaired by both countries' foreign ministers constituted in 2003, and a Bilateral Agreement on Cooperative Activities in the Field of Defence in 2001. Indonesia's export to India is rose to 22.25% in 2001 to 31.89% in 2016 and India's export to Indonesia is fluctuate as 14.38% in 2001 and grew maximum 20.50% in 2003 and 11.87%

in 2016. The downfall was registered due to prevailing global economic situation; fall in commodity prices and less overall imports by Indonesia. India is the second largest buyer of coal and crude palm oil from Indonesia and imports minerals, rubber, pulp and paper and hydrocarbons reserves. India exports refined petroleum products, maize, commercial vehicles, telecommunication equipment, oil seeds, animal feed, cotton, steel products and plastics to Indonesia.

MALAYSIA

India and Malaysia are also connected by various cultural and historical ties that date back to antiquity. The two countries are on excellently friendly terms with each other seeing as Malaysia is home to a strong concentration of Indian immigrants. Malaysia is India's third largest trading partner in ASEAN and India is the largest trading partner for Malaysia from among the countries of the South, excluding China. India-Malaysia defence relations have steadily grown over the years. Indian Air Force Training Team was deployed in Malaysia to train Malaysian pilots on the SU-30MKM aircraft from 2008 to 2010. Indian naval ships also make regular port calls in Malaysia; last visit was by the Eastern Fleet ships to Kemaman Port in June 2015. Malaysian Airlines flight MH 370 from Kuala Lumpur to Beijing on 8 March 2014, India extended all necessary assistance to the Malaysian authorities and deployed six ships and five aircrafts initially to undertake search operations in Bay of Bengal region and thereafter deployed two search and rescue aircrafts namely C130J and P8i in Subang Airport, Malaysia to assist in search operations. Five passengers in the flight were Indian nationals and the High Commission of India had provided necessary assistance to the families of the five passengers. Prime Minister Najib has expressed confidence that his two-day working visit to India to attend the ASEAN-India Commemorative Summit, will greatly improve ASEAN-India and Malaysia-India relations.

THAILAND

Thailand and India are cooperating in various multilateral fora like India's dialogue partnership with ASEAN, the ASEAN Regional Forum (ARF), and the East Asia Summit, the sub-regional grouping BIMSTEC involving Bangladesh, India, Sri Lanka, Thailand, Myanmar, Nepal and Bhutan, and trilateral transport linkages with Thailand, Myanmar and India. India is a member of the Asia Cooperation Dialogue (ACD) initiated by Thailand in 2002 and of the Mekong–Ganga Cooperation (MGC), a group of six countries. Since 2001 have witnessed growing warmth, increasing economic and commercial links, exchange of high-level visits on both sides, and the signing of a large number of Agreements leading to a further intensification of relations. India's 'Act East' policy is complemented by Thailand's 'Look West' policy in bringing the two nations closer. Sustained high level bilateral exchanges and regular meetings of bilateral institutional mechanisms have provided a major fillip to India-Thailand relations and achieved progress in key areas of cooperation such as security, defence, commerce, science and technology and education. In the ASEAN region, Thailand ranks as India's 4th largest trading partner after Singapore, Indonesia and Malaysia.

PHILIPPINES

Duterte and Modi exchanged economic and political views, including discussing the possibility of military cooperation. The defence relations of the two maritime nation-states have been marked by frequent visits by Indian navy warships and coast guard ships to the Philippines since 1998 and thereafter in 2017 under the terms of the 2006 Philippines-India Defence Cooperation Agreement. The Philippines and India should join hands and engage each other on many fronts. India's tremendous economic growth, it has optimized the production of computer software operating short- and intermediate-range ballistic missiles, nuclear capable aircraft, naval vessels, and India's active military space programme. Duterte's strategic visit to New Delhi, should gauge the possibilities for new engagement on defence. (Cabalza ,2018)

Expansion of Trade to East Asia

India has also established strong commercial, cultural and

military ties with the countries like Philippines, Singapore, Vietnam and Cambodia. India signed free trade agreements with Sri Lanka and Thailand and stepped up its military cooperation with them as well. It has forged various free trade agreements with East Asian economies, including a Comprehensive Economic Cooperation Agreement with Singapore and an Early Harvest Scheme with Thailand, while it is negotiating agreements with Japan, South Korea, and ASEAN member states. Ties have been strengthened with Taiwan, Japan and South Korea over common emphasis on democracy, human rights and strategic interests. South Korea and Japan remain amongst the major sources of foreign investment in India. A *People's Daily* editorial opined that the Look East Policy was "born out of the failure" of India's trying to play the Soviet Union and the United States against each other for its own benefit during the Cold War, and that trying to do the same with China and Japan by strengthening its ties with the latter would also fail. A columnist at the China Internet Information Centre criticized the Look East Policy as being born out of a misguided "fear of China" and as reflecting "a lack of understanding of the PLA's strategic ambitions".

Trade and Successive Summit

The East Asia Summit (EAS) is a forum held annually by leaders of, initially, 16 countries in the East Asian region, with a stated intention to increase this to 18 countries at the Sixth EAS in 2011. EAS meetings are held after annual ASEAN leaders' meetings. The first summit was held in Kuala Lumpur on December 14, 2005. The final report in 2002 of the East Asian Study Group, established by the ASEAN+3 countries, was based on an EAS involving ASEAN +3, therefore not involving Australia, New Zealand, or India. The EAS as proposed was to be an ASEAN-led development, with the summit to be linked to ASEAN summit meetings. However, the issue was to which countries beyond those in ASEAN the EAS was to be extended. The decision to hold the EAS was reached during the 2004 ASEAN plus three summit and the initial 16 members determined at the ASEAN plus Three Ministerial Meeting held in Laos at the end of July 2005.

India and the East Asian Summit

The inaugural East Asian Summit (EAS), touted as inventive commenced on December 14 in Kuala Lumpur comprising 16 nations— the 10 ASEAN countries, China, Japan, India, Australia and New Zealand with Russian President Vladimir Putin making a special appearance. The EAS Declaration, like many issued before in the region, is wide-ranging: from political and security cooperation, infrastructure development, financial issues, further liberalisation of regional trade and investment, poverty eradication to fighting epidemics. ASEAN has been holding plus three summit meetings since 1998 and India was also made a summit partner in 2002 but not included in the ASEAN+3 frameworks. As Indonesia will assume the chair of ASEAN in 2011 and will welcome the US and Russia for the first time to the East Asian Summit (EAS) or ASEAN plus 8, it will play a critical role in shaping the discourse and agenda of the region.

As a partial compromise, the governments of ASEAN + 3 agreed that each new member country would have to satisfy three criteria: it had to be a "dialogue partner" of ASEAN, it had to have signed ASEAN's Treaty of Amity and Cooperation (TAC), and it had to have significant economic involvement with the region. India was already a "dialogue partner" and had eagerly signed the TAC, but qualifying as a significant economic player required some persuasion. In the end, proponents of wider membership won the day. Not only India but also Australia and New Zealand are full members of the East Asian Summit. (Frost, 2009)

An invitation to India to the EAS now is recognition of its fast growing economic and political clout. The Look East Policy that New Delhi has been pursuing is entering a crucial phase after it helped build multi-faceted relations with ASEAN and other multilateral fora, and strengthen bilateral relations throughout the region encompassing political, defence/strategic and economic aspects. The EAS, representing nearly 50 percent of the world's population and over 20 percent of global trade, is a mega gathering and is a testimony to the rise of Asia and how rapidly the world's politico-economic equations are shifting. Even as the centre of gravity increasingly moves towards Asia, the 21st century will be dominated by events in terms of new economic dynamism as well as serious threats to global security. The bilateral trade between India and the countries of Southeast Asia clearly exhibits how these countries are economically coming closer to each other in spite of the fact that some countries of Southeast Asia are over-represented in terms of New Delhi's two-way trade relationship.

Look East Policy followed by Act East Policy (Present wave)

In the recent times India's foreign policy towards South East Asia has got a much added boost in International sphere. The Look East Policy has boosted up into a vibrant as 'Act East Policy'. Prime Minister Narendra Modi at the 12th ASEAN India Summit and the 9th East Asia Summit held in Nay Pyi Taw, Myanmar, in November, 2014, formally enunciated the Act East Policy. Due to the assertive rise of China, Act East Policy (AEP) has imparted greater vigor to India's ties with ASEAN. In particular, India has accorded a new focus on promoting connectivity through Myanmar and Thailand with other ASEAN states. Modi's allocation of $1 billion for promoting connectivity at the India-ASEAN Summit in Kuala Lumpur last November has brought the primacy of "connectivity, culture, and commerce" to the fore. India has recognised that success of AEP will be determined by its contribution to security and economic development of Northeast India. AEP has sought to significantly expand its geographical coverage beyond ASEAN alone, to include other countries like Japan, Australia, Pacific Island nations, South Korea, and Mongolia. (Sajjanhar, 2016) From a Look East to Act East perspective, it might be useful to recall a bit of past of India and ASEAN relationship. As many as 25 bilateral meetings with different leaders, besides attending multilateral summits, would be an explicit expression of India's **'Act East Policy'** and **'Make in India'** campaign being propagated by the Modi Government. The overall aim of this bilateral tour will be to better connectivity, highlight and discuss territorial, including maritime infringement, enhance trade and increase cooperation with the ASEAN and East Asian countries. Paradigm shift of India from **Look East** to **Act East Policy** is viewed as an affirmative step by the South East

Asian countries and displays a definitive eagerness and focus of the Indian Government towards meaningful cooperation in trade and other bilateral issues. An effective and timely pursuance of this initiative will help India to take a lead to reap out of proportion benefits from this region of unlimited opportunities. India's prime minister touched down for his first official visit to India's Northeast region. Narendra Modi's visit to the region helped further flesh out his strategy for reorienting India's foreign policy towards stronger ties with Southeast and East Asia. His initiatives seek to make good on Delhi's oft-repeated pledges to better integrate Northeast India with the rest of India and with its international neighbours. But to carry out his vision, he'll have to navigate a complex array of interests in the region, some of which, for a variety of reasons, are none too pleased with the plans Modi has set forth thus far.

MODI'S ACT EAST POLICY AND ITS IMPORTANCE

India's engagement with ASEAN is likely to become more comprehensive and strategic over time, the region would need to be prepared for the implications of India playing a more active role in regional affairs. One of the noticeable aspects of the Act East strategy has been the lack of any specific articulation about it from the Indian establishment. This could well be due to the strategy being an evolving one. Apart from its own evolution through the Indian strategic prism, Act East, clearly, is trying to take note of the rapid and complex developments in the region, particularly changes in the economic and security dynamics. (Palit, 2016) Accumulating all 10 heads of state or government of the Association of South East Asian Nations in Delhi, as chief guests for the Republic Day parade, is a big push for India's Act East policy. A similar situation looms today, as China's meteoric economic rise is transforming into Chinese assertiveness on territorial disputes in the region, together with other ways of undermining a multilateral rules-based order. As a result, despite ASEAN's deep economic engagements with China, the bloc doesn't want to put all its eggs in Beijing's basket. On India's part, boosting ties with ASEAN has multiple benefits. Not only is greater connectivity with the bloc crucial to developing India's northeast region, greater ASEAN investments into India can result in a multiplier effect across economic sectors. (TOI,2018) India's ties with ASEAN got a dose of both symbolism and substance. The ASEAN-India Commemorative Summit, followed by their attendance at the Republic Day parade as joint chief guests, underlined the new consensus on the need for Southeast Asia and India to boost cooperation. First, as the demand for goods in Western economies comes down, the region needs to look deeper within to grow markets and increase trade. Second, continuing tensions between the "great powers" — between the US and Russia, or the US and China — are forcing the unaligned countries of ASEAN and India to forge a common understanding. China's moves in particular, both its naval forays in the Indo-Pacific and its Belt and Road Initiative connectivity project, has the potential to change equations in the region. Third, as Singapore's Prime Minister and the Chairman of ASEAN, Lee Hsien Loong, reminded the world in an editorial, and Prime Minister Narendra Modi said in his speech at the summit, India's cultural and trade ties with Southeast Asia go back 2,000 years — and with Southeast Asia having come out of the overhang of Cold War divisions, India and ASEAN have a unique opportunity to reap the potential of their geographic proximity. (The Hindu, 2018)

Summary

To wind up this chapter it can be pointed out that some significant changes have taken place in the relation between India and SEA region especially during the 21st century. It is worth mentioning that during the period of cold war relation between India and SEA could not blossom. As a result there was no development of the LEP. Even during Mrs Gandhi's period India used to be misunderstood by many countries of SEA due to its closeness with former USSR. As a result India was not taken in to confidence in the formation of ASEAN. But the situation changed after Rajiv Gandhi became the Prime Minister. His visit to Indonesia, Thailand, Vietnam, Myanmar and ice breaking visit to China paved the way for better understanding. With the integration of Indian economy with the world economy after the collapse of the Soviet Union as the composite state, relations of

India with the SEA and EA neighbours opened up. India had to remove the restrictions on the trade and adopted of LPG leading to formation of a framework of India's LEP. India's exports to the ASEAN in proportion to the world exports increased from 7.6% in 2001 to 11.4% in 2011 however there is some fluctuation in recent years. In 2016 it stands at 10.1%. India's imports from ASEAN have increased from 8.6% in 2001 to 10.7% in 2016. The Narasimha Rao's Look East Policy has boosted up into a vibrant as Narendra Modi's 'Act East Policy'. Paradigm shift of India from **Look East** to **Act East Policy** is viewed as an affirmative step by the South East Asian countries and displays a definitive eagerness and focus of the Indian Government towards meaningful cooperation in trade and other bilateral issues. The Act East Policy has sought to significantly expand its geographical coverage beyond ASEAN alone, to include other nations like Japan, Australia, Pacific Island nations, South Korea and Mongolia.

Chapter - III

Russia's Growing Interest and Relation with South-East Asian Countries

Historic Relation of Russia and South East Asian Nations

Russia's role in Southeast Asia is considered as an indicator of the new system of international relations. Historically, Russia has not had a strong bond with Southeast Asian nations due to past Cold War suspicions but Vietnam being the major exception to this imperative. Of course there is no longer any basis for the intense political suspicion and fear that marked the relationship between Moscow and Southeast Asia during the Cold War when Southeast Asia presented a spectacle of one of the most violent and bitterly contested zones of international rivalry. Russia was no longer considered as a threat by ASEAN. At present no critical security problems characterise the relations between Southeast Asia and Russia. The nations of Southeast Asia have occupied varying levels of interest in Soviet foreign policy since the Bolshevik revolution. Only a few countries in the region, such as Indonesia and Vietnam, established early contacts with the Soviet Union while the rest were either still under colonialism or were not willing to develop contacts with a communist regime. The 1960s and 1970s witnessed a greater level of interaction by Moscow with several Southeast Asian states. Soviet relations with ASEAN and the rest of Southeast Asia reached a high point during the Gorbachev period. Since the decline of the Soviet Union, Russia's foreign policy has evolved from a Western-oriented one to a multi-dimensional one, with a stronger focus on Southeast Asia. Soviet Union's alliance with

Vietnam, was viewed by ASEAN members to varying degrees as a threat, increasingly so in the wake of Vietnamese expansion into Laos and Cambodia. During the early post-Soviet years the Asia-Pacific region again became peripheral to Russian foreign policy. Immediately after the Soviet break-up in 1991, there was an enthusiastic search by some member states of ASEAN and the CIS for a new relationship void of ideology. (Thambipillai,1994) The most important strategic goal of Russia's foreign policy in Asia is to become involved in regional integration to have more opportunities. In fact, relations with ASEAN started from zero. The role of Southeast Asia in Russian foreign policy was uncertain in the beginning of the 1990s but after that it is slowly revived. The Association of South East Asian Nations (ASEAN) is the oldest and one of the most successful organisations in the region. The significance of ASEAN for Russia is obvious. The cooperation of Russia and Southeast Asia continue for a long time in shape of development of the relation in structure of stability and safety, economic, and also social and cultural cooperation. Attraction to an ASEAN is the main concern in development of the Russian foreign policy presently because the ASEAN is "a backbone element of a regional order". (Klyuchanskaya, 2011)

Russia and ASEAN Partnership

Russia and ASEAN dialogue was started on July 1991 when Russian representatives were invited by the Malaysian Government to attend an ASEAN Ministerial Meeting. In March 1993, the foreign visits of Vice-President Alexander Rutskoi had led a delegation to Malaysia and Singapore to boost economic co-operation and seek joint ventures. He was a general and ex-pilot in the Soviet air force, made his first trip to Southeast Asia at a time when he was regarded as a potential successor to Yeltsin. The high profile visit was partly for domestic purposes, but was also significant in the sense that, being a fighter pilot, he was an important link to the potential sale of MiG-29 fighter aircraft to Malaysia and other likely buyers of Russian jets in the region. The economic implications were also manifest as he was accompanied by the Minister of Foreign Economic Relations and the Minister of Agriculture. Rutskoi was the highest ranking Russian (or for that matter Soviet) official to visit Malaysia or Singapore and thus created diplomatic history. In Malaysia, he discussed co-operation in aerospace technology and palm oil refining. (Lissovolik, 2012). Russia was subsequently elevated to a full Dialogue Partner of ASEAN in July 1996 at the 29th ASEAN Ministerial Meeting in Jakarta, Indonesia. Before Putin formed govt. there were a lot of purpose no doubt but there was an absence of practical action, a situation which began to improve after Putin's assumption of office. It appears that under President Putin, the understanding about the need for a more diversified approach to foreign economic policy and for building stronger ties with Asia has grown in the upper echelons of power. The above background demonstrates that the relation among Russia and South East Asian nations is not new, but this chapter mainly highlights how old association is revitalised by the resurgent Russia.

Resurgent Russia's Relation with South-East Asian states: Period of Putin

Russia's Foreign Policy under President Vladimir Putin emphasised to promote economic interests in Asia and in Southeast Asia. He held office from 2000 to 2008, and assumed power again in 2012 till date. For fourth time he has adorned the office of the president. Putin was once known as a classic economic reformer. Russia was devastated by a financial crisis twice a decade prior to his assumption of office as the President in 2000 for the first time. Putin pushed major economic reforms to integrate Russia in to Europe. Then Putin the economic reformer gave way to Putin, the nationalist. A different side of Putin has emerged on the domestic economic front, cautious and responsible, focused on stability and reform controlling inflation rather than stimulating growth. Abroad he remains aggressive. (Sharma, 2018) In the mid-2000s Russia was gradually mastering the resources to develop relations with geographically remote regions. At the same time, Russia's role as a champion of multi-polarity began to grow. It can be said that Putin made multipolarity the center of his foreign policy. The development of relations with ASEAN looked like a natural element of that policy. Policies enunciated by Gorbachev to promote better economic and political relations with Asian countries and to withdraw active support for Vietnam started bearing fruit. In the regional relation of South East Asia Soviet Union came to be accepted as cooperative partner. It was necessary for Russia to join the regional integration process in the early stages to avoid its exclusion from the region again. In both positive and negative terms China has been closely connected with ASEAN both geopolitically and economically. So there is a need for more action if Russia is to "catch up" with current Chinese interests' vis-à-vis the region. (Thambipillai, 1994) However the changing environment, of International system is seeking to expand the new linkages in political and economic sphere of Russian Federation on the one hand and South East Asian Nations on the other. Russia's diplomatic overtures toward Cambodia are a crucial step towards establishing Moscow as a major player in the ASEAN trade bloc. Ultimately though, the success of Russia's outreach will depend on Putin's ability to overcome Cambodian disdain for Moscow's alliance with Vietnam and Cambodia's willingness to make sweeping economic reforms that will bolster its viability as a trade partner. (Ramani, 2016)

POLITICAL RELATIONS

The nature of domestic politics within the Russian Federation is a major factor in explaining that country's relationship with the Southeast Asian Region. Its foreign policy has become a hostage of domestic politics, for whenever there is internal instability; foreign policy is affected, sometimes neglected, especially in the lowest priority areas. Contemporary Russia has also been in response to Russian behaviour. Most of the leaders in the region are not prepared to respond to the rapid changes in Russia as they are still uncertain how to accept the new Russia, having been conditioned by the Russian "threat" for about half a century. For a long time, Russia's relations with ASEAN had been limited to the political sphere.

More than half of ASEAN's members have purchased arms from Russia's revitalised defence industry and sought its expertise in the energy sector. Vietnam is the most befitting example.

Vietnam's armed forces are equipped predominantly with Russian weaponry, including frigates, fighter jets, missiles and submarines. Russia is also building the country's first nuclear power plant. But after two decades, the relationship is yet to achieve even a fraction of its full potential. Because of this, ASEAN demurely refused Moscow's request to upgrade their relationship from partnership to strategic partner (the status of America, China and Japan) until Russia ups its game in Southeast Asia. Such are the conditions clearly spelt out in the Sochi Declaration, as well as the action plan that ASEAN and Russia issued at the summit. In the area of politics and security, the two sides, however promised to intensify cooperation in the fight against international terrorism and transnational crime. The provisions on the South China Sea dispute are fixed at the lowest common denominator, with calls for all parties to abide by international law and an early conclusion to the Code of Conduct. (Tsvetov, 2016) Diplomatic influence without the underlying economic basis was a correct description of Russia's policy toward ASEAN in the 1990s. Despite the fact that political partnership had been on the rise during that decade, little progress was made in the field of economic cooperation. Ultimately, traditionally weak economic links between Russia and Southeast Asia also obstructed Russia's search for influence. (Rangsimaporn, 2009) Russia's accession to the Treaty of Amity and Cooperation in Southeast Asia (1976) on 29 November 2004 turned out to be a milestone in ASEAN — Russia dialogue relations. ASEAN and Russia maintain good political and security cooperation relations. This document serves as a political declaration on the norms and principles of relations among countries in the region and includes the obligation that the contracting parties are not to participate in any manner or form in any activity which may constitute a threat to the political and economic stability of another contracting party.

Russia's accession to the TAC reflects her strong commitment to regional peace, stability and a significant contribution to the TAC as an important code of conduct governing inter-states relations. Russia participates in a series of consultative meetings with ASEAN under the ASEAN-Russia dialogue relations to discuss and exchange views on political and security issues of mutual interest and concern. These include ministerial meetings, senior officials' meetings and meetings at expert level, as well as dialogue and cooperation frameworks initiated by ASEAN, such as the ASEAN Regional Forum (ARF), the Post Ministerial Conferences (PMCs) Plus One, ASEAN Defence Ministers' Meeting Plus and the East Asia Summit.

ASEAN-Russia Summit

The key areas of cooperation between Russia and the ASEAN Member States were set out in the Agreement between the Governments of the Member States of the Association of Southeast Asian Nations and the Government of the Russian Federation on Economic and Development Cooperation that was signed in 2005 during the leaders' meeting in Kuala Lumpur. This is the first ASEAN-Russia Summit held on December 13, 2005. It was a landmark in Russia's relations with this Association. The Agreement ensures favourable conditions for promoting economic cooperation as well as cooperation in trade, investment, research, technology and culture. The first Summit was attended by Vladimir Putin the President of the Russian Federation, Sultan Haji Hassanal Bolkiah Mu'izzaddin Waddaulah of Brunei Darussalam, Hun Sen, the Prime Minister of the Kingdom of Cambodia Hun Sen, President of the Republic of Indonesia Susilo Bambang Yudhoyono, Prime Minister of the Lao People's Democratic Republic Bounnhang Vorachith, Prime Minister of Malaysia Abdullah bin Haji Ahmad Badawi, Prime Minister of the Republic of the Union of Myanmar Soe Win, President of the Republic of the Philippines Gloria Macapagal Arroyo, Prime Minister of the Republic of Singapore Lee Hsien Loong, Prime Minister of the Kingdom of Thailand Thaksin Shinawatra, and Phan Vãn Khis the Prime Minister of the Socialist Republic of Vietnam. Participants in the summit discussed a broad range of economic and political cooperation issues. The ten member nations of the Association of Southeast Asian Nations hold out a massive economic prospect for Russia. That meeting identified the priority areas of their interaction and kick-started practical work on a broad range of issues. It should be recognised that for various objective and subjective reasons Russia's economic cooperation with the Association had been for a long time mostly skin deep, and even today it fails to keep up with the pace of the political dialogue. (Sumsky, 2011) The Comprehensive Programme of Action to Promote Cooperation between the Association of Southeast Asian Nations and the Russian Federation 2005-2015, was adopted on 13 December 2005 to strengthen and promote ASEAN — Russia dialogue, with the parties approving a roadmap for the implementation of this programme.

The second ASEAN — Russia Summit took place in Hanoi (Vietnam) on 30 October 2010. Russia was represented by President Dmitry Medvedev. Minister of Foreign Affairs of the Russian Federation Sergei Lavrov also attended the summit. Mr Lavrov mentioned in his speech that at the first summit the ASEAN countries displayed special interest in the nuclear power industry, considering Russia's vast experience in this area. He also said that the sides reviewed the development of cooperation in countering organised crime and drug trafficking. At the second Summit, Russia and ASEAN reaffirmed their commitment to the consolidation and steady development of their comprehensive partnership with a view to raising their relations to a higher level. Apart from political dimension of Russia-ASEAN countries relations, it's important to have a clear understanding of the economic ties that bring them together. Though these economic projects are not as prominent as Russia-Europe or Russia-China ones, they are still expanding step by step. From joint railways blueprints to information technology exchange, Russia and ASEAN have a clear and long road ahead of them in terms of mutual economic development.

ECONOMIC COOPERATION

ASEAN-Russia economic cooperation has been stronger through regular dialogue and engagement such as the Senior Economic Officials Meeting (SEOM)-Russia Consultations and the ASEAN Economic Ministers-Russia Consultations. At the 6th AEM-Russia Consultations held on 11 September 2017, the Ministers endorsed the revised ASEAN-Russia Trade and Investment Cooperation Roadmap, along with its Post-2017 ASEAN-Russia Trade and Investment Cooperation Work Programme, which was built upon positive developments made under the Post-2015 Work Programme. The Post-2017 Work Programme covers, among others, regular dialogues as well as various projects in the spheres of technology, food and agriculture, transport, energy, tourism, and small and medium sized enterprises (SMEs), and promoting business-to-business contacts.

Russia's economic presence in the SEA is distinctive in respect of three areas in which Russia has traditionally been strong: oil and gas, nuclear power and military-technical cooperation. Energy is viewed as a promising area for cooperation between ASEAN and Russia. Activities to establish international collaboration between scientists/experts from Russia and ASEAN Member States for joint initiatives in the field of renewable energy were successfully implemented in 2015/2016. Despite Russia's economic presence in the region being not consistent, arms and military equipment have always been among the best-selling Russian products in the SEA market. The fact that Vietnam individually and as part of SEA, was mentioned in the foreign policy strategy was viewed by experts as a landmark and great hopes were pinned on a new course and a qualitative change in Russia-ASEAN relations. Historically Vietnam has been and remains the largest buyer. (Tsvetov, 2016) The organisation's "economic tigers," namely, Malaysia, Singapore, and Thailand, were seen as potentially significant trading partners as well as economic models that Russia could imitate. It is commented that ASEAN is facing the task of searching for a new identity in the emerging multi-polar world and consolidating its role in regional integration processes as new power centers emerge in the Asia-Pacific. (Jinda, 2017)

GROWING INTEREST OF RUSSIA AND SEA

Russia's interest in SEA in the 2000s waxed and waned, as witnessed by the sporadic nature of Russia-ASEAN meetings. Malaysia ordered some aircraft and recent reports speak of possible expansion of sales to Thailand. In the late 2000s and early 2010s Myanmar bought several MiG fighters, and cooperation with the country is likely to continue. Since then only one important Russian foreign policy document meaningfully mentioned SEA, and that was the Russian President's Address to the Federal Assembly in

2015. In that address Vladimir Putin referred to the (Eurasian Economic Union) EEU-Vietnam Free Trade Zone created that same year and mentioned the Russia-ASEAN summit in Sochi in May 2016. He also proposed creating the EEU-SCO (Shanghai Cooperation Organisation)-ASEAN "economic partnership" that would concentrate on "protecting investments, optimizing the movement of goods across borders, joint development of technical standards for the next-generation products and mutual opening of access to the markets of services and capitals." Meanwhile the question of real interaction between Russia and SEA countries remains open. The 20th anniversary of the Russia-ASEAN Dialogue Partnership in 2016 is a good occasion to investigate new sources of development for Russian-ASEAN relations. ASEAN-Russia cooperation is now being undertaken under the framework of the Comprehensive Programme of Actions (CPA) to Promote Cooperation between ASEAN and the Russian Federation 2016-2020, which was adopted by the Foreign Ministers of ASEAN and Russia on the occasion of the Commemorative Summit in May 2016 to succeed the CPA 2005-2015. The CPA (2016-2020) is aimed at promoting and enhancing ASEAN-Russia Dialogue Relations through assisting ASEAN in its efforts in regional economic integration and Community building. The strong point of the Russian economic existence in Southeast Asia lies in oil and gas, nuclear energy, and military technology. Singapore and Malaysia currently buy Russian oil and Indonesia is also involved in several energy projects, but again it is Vietnam that is Russia's chief oil and gas partner, with projects in both Vietnam and Russia. The same is true of nuclear energy. Russia has nuclear power construction projects in Myanmar and Thailand, but its main project is building the Ninh Thuan-1 nuclear power plant in southern Vietnam, where it is also providing related services and training personnel. Russian weapons are still the hottest commodity on Southeast Asian markets. Again, Vietnam has historically been and still remains the region's largest buyer of Russian arms. Its significant acquisitions include fighter jets, frigates, anti-ship missiles, missile defence systems, and Varshavyanka submarines (the last of these submarines will be delivered to Vietnam in late 2016). Indonesia, Malaysia, Thailand, and Myanmar have also purchased Russian weapons, although in smaller quantities. Major purchases from Russia include fighter planes, frigates, anti-ship missiles, air defence systems and Kilo-class submarines, the last of which were to be delivered to Vietnam in late 2016. Vietnamese shipyards are also assembling Tarantula corvettes under a Russian license. Indonesia also buys Russian military hardware, including armored personnel carriers, helicopters and fighter planes. (Tsvetov, 2016) Russia-ASEAN trade shows to have grown at an notable rate in the last decade—but only from a low starting point. The volume of trade increased five-fold from 2005 to 2014.

RUSSIA AND ASEAN TRADE RELATION

Russian economy received a jolt in the wake of the demise of communism. The resurgent Russia, however, picked up momentum and started doing business around the world including with South East Asia or ASEAN. The following table reflects the Russian exports to ASEAN and imports from ASEAN in absolute terms i.e. in dollar as well as in percent showing the proportion of Russia's export and import relation with ASEAN in the context of total exports and imports status with the world.

In the 21st century Russia-ASEAN trade appears to have grown at an impressive rate with exports growing at a rate of 14.87% and imports growing at 20.05%. Russia's trade relation in terms of exports and imports as a proportion of its trade with the world has not been very significant, varying between 0.65% to 1.95%. In most of the period imports size has been more than exports. From the study period of sixteen years, there has been a negative trade balance in eight years. From 2001 to 2005, there was a positive trade balance, but since 2005 there has been negative trade balance except in 2010, 2011, 2012. In the years 2015 and 2016, the percentage of imports from ASEAN in proportion to total imports from the world has gone above 4%, causing a larger trade deficit. Russia's trade relations with the ASEAN nations have not been very affirmative. However, in spite of a history of Cold War suspicion, at present the trade relations between Russia and some member countries of ASEAN have gained momentum.

Table 3.1: Russia's Export, Import and Trade Balance with ASEAN

Unit -Thousand USD

	Russia's Export To ASEAN			Russia's Import From ASEAN			
Year	**World**	**ASEAN**	**%**	**World**	**ASEAN**	**%**	**Trade Balance**
2001	99868397	1197286	1.20%	41865362	576552	1.38%	620734
2002	106691998	1510597	1.42%	46176985	833777	1.81%	676820
2003	133655685	1503703	1.13%	57345988	992896	1.73%	510807
2004	181600379	1777346	0.98%	75569015	1315950	1.74%	461396
2005	241451657	2159188	0.89%	98707256	2046720	2.07%	112468
2006	301550666	1959779	0.65%	137811060	2759584	2.00%	-799805
2007	352266399	2563296	0.73%	199725955	4251889	2.13%	-1688593
2008	467993955	4371332	0.93%	267051244	5784301	2.17%	-1412969
2009	301796059	3607525	1.20%	170826590	4297428	2.52%	-689903
2010	397067521	6513607	1.64%	228911658	5553979	2.43%	959628
2011	516992618	7857342	1.52%	306091490	7584705	2.48%	272637
2012	524766421	7305484	1.39%	316192918	8297211	2.62%	-991727
2013	527265919	8490895	1.61%	314945095	8986358	2.85%	-495463
2014	497833529	11796276	2.37%	286648777	8781659	3.06%	3014617
2015	343907652	5352480	1.56%	182781965	7304524	4.00%	-1952044
2016	285491052	5566876	1.95%	182261656	8001965	4.39%	-2435089
CAGR	9.7%	14.87%		12.91%	20.05%		

Source: http://www.trademap.org/stDataSources

It is found that after 2009 the export of Russia has not increased significantly in comparison with import from ASEAN. Here one finds that Russia's import from ASEAN has grown impressively which was 1.38% in 2001 and which touched 4.39% in 2016.The above figure proves positive trade relation between Russia and ASEAN because Russia's import from the ASEAN is higher than export to it. The above figures also focus on CAGR (Compound Annual Growth Rate) of Russia's export to and import from world in comparison with ASEAN. Here the important finding is that the CAGR of Russia's import from ASEAN is higher than export to it. Russia's growth rate in connection with import from ASEAN is 20.05% and export to ASEAN is 14.87%.

Russia and Member states of ASEAN

The Association of South East Asian Nations (ASEAN) is the successful organisation in the region. The strategic importance of ASEAN is also determined by its role as the main driving force of integration in the Asia-Pacific region (APR). Though in the past, Russia has not had a strong association with Southeast Asian countries but Vietnam, Cambodia, and Laos had been cold-war allies of the Soviet Union prior to their inclusion in ASEAN. After

Table 3.2: Trend and growth of Russia's exports to various ASEAN nations during 2001-16

	ASEAN	Singapore	Vietnam	Malaysia	Thailand	Indonesia	Philippines	Myanmar	Cambodia	Brunei Darussalam	Laos
Year	Thousand USD	%	%	%	%	%	%	%	%	%	%
2001	1197286	47.99	13.60	22.49	5.96	2.60	3.86	2.79	0.40	0.00	0.31
2002	1510597	34.55	21.28	23.01	6.36	2.03	6.47	5.82	0.22	0.00	0.27
2003	1503703	10.52	23.75	28.27	8.67	15.67	12.19	0.71	0.07	0.00	0.15
2004	1777346	10.68	39.81	6.43	20.96	8.18	12.19	1.31	0.09	0.00	0.36
2005	2159188	14.32	34.22	6.95	25.32	9.38	9.17	0.03	0.11	0.00	0.50
2006	1959779	40.33	15.49	12.21	17.71	9.54	4.04	0.33	0.15	0.00	0.18
2007	2563296	42.44	18.91	10.47	12.76	9.78	4.58	0.57	0.44	0.00	0.07
2008	4371332	27.00	13.29	10.78	28.19	14.10	5.56	0.74	0.20	0.02	0.13
2009	3607525	36.78	24.09	6.02	12.18	7.85	11.28	1.26	0.26	0.00	0.28
2010	6513607	30.83	17.21	5.29	23.58	10.21	11.72	0.96	0.09	0.00	0.11
2011	7857342	28.64	12.86	5.31	26.70	7.38	15.50	3.44	0.05	0.01	0.13
2012	7305484	21.76	19.01	3.78	19.32	17.93	16.20	1.79	0.08	0.00	0.13
2013	8490895	22.21	16.18	15.08	14.99	14.53	15.59	0.93	0.06	0.00	0.44
2014	11796276	47.06	5.46	15.43	14.85	7.78	8.98		0.03	0.00	0.07
2015	5352480	46.56	15.40	11.87	9.74	8.21	6.00	1.83	0.08	0.01	0.29
2016	5566876	32.27	24.66	17.46	11.07	7.25	2.62	4.29	0.14	0.00	0.24
CAGR	**14.87%**	**18.57**	**10.84**	**11.14**	**18.11**	**20.73**	**15.94**	**18.64**	**6.46**		**11.83**

Source: http://www.trademap.org/stDataSources

the dissolution of the Soviet Union under President Boris Yeltsin's leadership, Russia lost its position even in countries where it previously had influence. In the beginning of the 1990s the role of Southeast Asia in Russian foreign policy was uncertain. Subsequently, Russia-ASEAN dialogue partnership could materialise. However, Russia's failure in actively participating in banking and investment cooperation with ASEAN states is clearly noticeable. The number of joint ventures is relatively few. Till now the Vietnam-Russia Joint Venture Bank, founded in 2009, is the sole institution of cooperation. Adequate attention is not given by the Russian state structures to the needs of private enterprise.

The Table 3.2 presents Russia's exports to ten member countries of ASEAN. However, among all ASEAN member countries five top export destination of Russia are Singapore, Malaysia, Vietnam, Indonesia, Thailand. Singapore is the first export destination in comparison to other ASEAN member nations during the period 2001-16. Singapore is the nation with whom Russia has the highest percentage of exports of total exports to ASEAN countries followed by Malaysia, Vietnam, Indonesia, Thailand respectively. The compound growth rates of total export is to Indonesia, Singapore, Myanmar, Thailand, Philippines are 20.73%,18.57%, 18.64%, 18.11%,15.94% respectively which is more than the CAGR of total exports to ASEAN,i.e.14.87%. Many scholars remained skeptical about the prospects for cooperation between Russia and ASEAN. The two sides have, however, been increasing their economic ties over last several years, creating a comprehensive agenda and a legal platform for partnership. ASEAN is seen as a rising center of power in Asia. A solid relationship could provide a greater balance in Russia's Asia policy, bolstering the multipolarity that ensures continuing Russian influence in world affairs in the face of American predominance.

The ASEAN market holds much potential for Russia to project influence through its primary economic assets-arms and energy and for further expansion and diversification of economic ties. ASEAN is a diversified entity whose members Russia assigns different layers of priority to. Each country carries its own significance in Russia's quest for regional influence, so Russian

Table 3.3: Trend and growth of Russia's import from ASEAN Nations during 2001-16

Year	ASEAN	Singapore	Vietnam	Malaysia	Thailand	Indonesia	Philippines	Myanmar	Cambodia	Brunei	Laos
		%	%	%	%	%	%	%	%	%	%
2001	576552	18.95	13.88	28.02	18.58	16.67	3.84	0.02	0.03	0	0.01
2002	833777	10.60	9.76	27.59	27.26	19.48	3.69	1.55	0.04	0.00	0.02
2003	992896	9.12	7.76	30.24	30.39	18.42	3.95	0.03	0.06	0	0.02
2004	1315950	12.28	7.64	32.17	27.00	16.79	3.80	0.13	0.18	0	0.02
2005	2046720	15.50	8.51	32.88	22.08	17.06	3.58	0.11	0.27	0	0.02
2006	2759584	15.81	12.67	32.41	20.28	15.23	3.18	0.11	0.28	0.00	0.02
2007	4251889	10.64	12.28	34.42	23.62	15.63	2.92	0.06	0.42	2.35E-05	0.02
2008	5784301	8.04	14.71	34.12	25.88	13.72	2.96	0.10	0.44	1.73E-05	0.02
2009	4297428	16.13	16.14	26.47	21.69	14.91	3.87	0.11	0.68	6.98E-05	0.01
2010	5553979	5.98	20.00	24.18	24.67	18.83	5.47	0.26	0.61	0.0	0.01
2011	75844705	0.51	2.27	2.00	2.55	2.02	0.53	0.03	0.09	0	0.00
2012	8297211	4.99	27.40	17.73	23.75	18.94	5.59	0.51	1.07	0.09	0.02
2013	8986358	6.15	28.90	15.64	23.19	19.22	5.06	0.39	1.43	2.23E-05	0.02
2014	8781659	6.86	26.14	16.61	25.41	18.76	4.31	0.41	1.47	4.55E-05	0.02
2015	7304524	7.06	28.14	18.11	20.47	20.87	3.67	0.22	1.46	8.21E-05	0.01
2016	8001965	6.20	30.81	15.05	14.33	27.65	3.68	0.24	1.70	0	0.35
CAGR	**22.1%**	**12.19%**	**31.84%**	**13.87%**	**18.41%**	**22.31%**	**21.93%**	**32.79%**	**55.95%**	**3.24%**	**29.63%**

Source: http://www.trademap.org/stDataSources

considers that Southeast Asia is the region for developing policy such "New Player" in this region and with the ASEAN members. (Jinda, 2017) Russia is also finding an unlikely market in ASEAN for Russian oil and gas. Tightening Western sanctions have left Russia looking for alternative export destinations. Thailand has seized the opportunity to diversify its energy sources. Russian energy exports to ASEAN have increased five-fold since 2013. ASEAN represents a host of opportunities for Russia. The increasing military ties gas exports to the region is the beginning. Putin will likely to use these successes to further Russian interests. Russian businesses will use the MOUs to gain valuable inroads into new markets. Russia will find ASEAN a willing recipient of exports, investment and military equipment. This is the beginning of Russia's push to become a committed player in Southeast Asia. (ASEAN Today, 2018)

ASEAN nations are increasingly turning to Russia to meet their arms procurement needs. Russia now sells 43.1% of its weapons to Asia. Between 2000 and 2016, Vietnam imported more than 80% of its arms from Russia. Both Myanmar and Laos bought between 60% and 80% of their weapons from Russia. One of Russia's main export destinations within Asia besides China and India is Vietnam which imported 10 percent of Russia's total arms exports between 2010 and 2016. (Gnanasagaran, 2018)

Putin has increasingly turned his attention to Asia in general and South East Asia in particular. The ten member nations of the Association of Southeast Asian Nations present an enormous economic opportunity for Russia. The strength of the Russian economic presence in Southeast Asia lies in oil and gas, nuclear energy, and military technology. Singapore and Malaysia currently buy Russian oil and Indonesia is also involved in several energy projects, but again it is Vietnam that is Russia's chief oil and gas partner, with projects in both Vietnam and Russia. The same is true of nuclear energy. (Tsvetov, 2016)

As discussed earlier (Table 3.1) Russia's import from ASEAN has grown impressively which was 1.38% in 2001 and which touched 4.39% in 2016. But the Table 3.2 presents Russia's import from ten members States of ASEAN. Among ASEAN member's nation Vietnam and Indonesia played major role in case of Russia's import from these countries. During 2001 Russia's import from Vietnam was 13.88% and it has come down to 2.27% in 2011. But after this year this rate is increasing at very impressive rate i.e. 27.40% in 2012 to 30.81% in 2016.

In April of this year Russia agreed to a new deal with Vietnam for closer military ties between the two countries. The military roadmap will last until 2020. It will see Russian naval vessels based in Vietnam for use in search and rescue missions. The two countries will conduct joint training exercises. 176 Vietnamese soldiers will also travel to Moscow for training. There have also been considerable developments in the Russia-Laos military relationship. In March, plans of a new Russian military facility in Laos surfaced. The facility in Vientiane will provide technical assistance to the Laotian military. The Laos military uses Russian-made equipment. The Russian government will base a team of staff in Vientiane to provide training and help. Russian Defence Minister, Sergey Shoygu, visited Laos earlier this year. During his visit, the two countries discussed ways to deepen military cooperation.

It is no surprise ASEAN countries are turning to Russia. Russia will also provide the 11 SU-35 jets for Yuyu Sutisna's fleet in Indonesia. As part of the deal, Russia will buy palm oil, coffee and tea from Indonesia. Russian Foreign Minister Sergei Lavrov toured Southeast Asia in 2017. He also promised to provide "significant favourable conditions" for Indonesian exports to Russia. (ASEAN Today, 2018) Indonesia, Malaysia, Vietnam, Thailand and the Philippines — have been identified as frontrunners to establish civilian nuclear power programmes in the region. These five states are considered frontrunners due to their more advanced legal and regulatory frameworks, nuclear energy infrastructures, and developed organisation and human resources. These criteria are among the 19 nuclear infrastructure issues that are outlined in the International Atomic Energy Agency (IAEA) Milestones Approach to nuclear infrastructure development. ASEAN member states, Laos, Cambodia, and Myanmar have not ruled out the use of nuclear power but they have not committed to any specific infrastructure development plans and implementation timelines. However, all three have signed bilateral agreements with Russia on nuclear power cooperation. (Putra, 2018)

Regional Economic Organisations

Before the presentation of specific quantitative data relating to trade between India and Russia with different prominent regional organisations in the form of tables, it is necessary to introduce the different organisations.

SAARC (South Asian Association for Regional Cooperation)

SAARC is the regional intergovernmental organisation and geopolitical union of nations in South Asia. Its member states are Afghanistan, Bangladesh, Bhutan, India, Pakistan, the Maldives, Nepal and Sri Lanka. SAARC was founded by seven states in 1985. It was initiated in Dhaka on 8 December 1985. In the declaration of the Seventh SAARC Summit in April, in Dhaka, Bangladesh, the Member States highlighted noted a number of recent positive developments in the area of nuclear, chemical, and conventional disarmament, including the agreements on bilateral arms reductions with Russia. Moscow in January 1993 would be successfully carried out. Russia has applied for observer status membership of SAARC.

SAARC, as a regional forum, has great potential, but this potential of regional cooperation cannot be realised without strong bilateral linkages. Given the asymmetry inherent in the geographical, economic and strategic dimensions of the eight member countries, meaningful cooperation can materialise only when there is mutual trust and willingness among member countries to resolve and overcome bilateral differences and apprehensions for the greater good of their own people. India has a major responsibility in this respect on account of several factors. More importantly, India should take initiatives to sort out the differences which the partner countries have been experiencing in trade with India on matters relating to border trade and transit facilities.

PM Modi plans to set up a SAARC Bank, on the lines of the BRICS Bank, to take forward his South Asia initiative. This attempt is expected go a long way in facilitating regional economic development through financing of infrastructure for trade in goods and services and boost up investment in the region. SAARC maintains permanent diplomatic relations at the United Nations as an observer and has developed links with multilateral entities, including the European Union.

EU (European Union)

The European Union (EU) is a political and economic union of 28 member states that are located primarily in Europe. The EU was created by the Maastricht Treaty, which entered into force on November 1, 1993. The European Union is the second largest economy in the world in nominal terms and as per to purchasing power parity (PPP). The 12th EU-India summit confirms that EU and India are strengthening and readjusting their partnership in its political dimension, thus pushing bringing our relationship to new heights.

Relations between the Republic of India and the European Union are currently defined by the 1994 EU-India Cooperation Agreement. The EU is a notable trade partner for India and the two sides have been attempting to negotiate a free trade deal since 2007. India is the EU's 9th largest trading partner with 2.4% of the EU's overall trade. Talks on an EU-India Bilateral Trade and Investment Agreement have stalled after failing to resolve differences related to matters such as the level of FDI and market access, manufacture of generic drugs, greenhouse gas emissions, civil nuclear energy, farming subsidies, regulation and safeguards of the financial sector, cooperation on tax evasion, overseas financing of NGOs in India, trade controls, technology transfer restrictions and cooperation on embargoes.

Russian–European relations are the international relations between the European Union (EU) and its largest bordering state, Russia, to the east. The relations of individual member states of the European Union and Russia vary, though a 1990s common foreign policy outline towards Russia was the first such EU foreign policy agreed. Furthermore, four European Union-Russia Common Spaces are agreed as a framework for promoting better relations. The latest EU-Russia strategic partnership was signed in 2011.

APEC (Asia-Pacific Economic Cooperation)

APEC is a forum for 21 Pacific Rim member economies that promotes free trade throughout the Asia-Pacific region. It was established in 1989 in response to the growing interdependence of Asia-Pacific economies and the advent of regional trade blocs in other parts of the world; to allay fears that highly industrialised Japan (a member of G7) would come to dominate economic activity in the Asia-Pacific region; and to set up new markets for agricultural products and raw materials beyond Europe. APEC functions as a cooperative, multilateral economic and trade forum. Member economies participate on the basis of open dialogue and respect for views of all participants. India's membership in APEC would be an important step towards India opening to increased trade and investment and preparing for inclusion in trade pacts like the TPP, which will promote future regional commerce. Moreover, by admitting India, APEC could pave the way for a more inclusive trade agenda in the region. An APEC that includes India will generate economic benefits for India and the other APEC member economies, as well as help promote greater international cooperation. (Gupta, 2015)

India, along with Russia, Vietnam and Peru, has been one of the leading countries which have tried hard to become a member of APEC. The APEC leaders decision not to admit India in the recent expansion at Vancouver while admitting Russia, Vietnam and Peru, and the imposition of a moratorium for another ten years on inclusion of new members has not only come as a rude shock to New Delhi, but it is a major setback to India's 'Look East policy.' Apart from the South Asian Association for Regional Cooperation (SAARC), India is the only major country in the world which is yet to become a member of a regional free trading club. Given the enormous political problems, especially between India and Pakistan, India's allegedly domineering position in South Asia and a number of other economic constraints, SAARC is not expected to make much headway. In any case SAARC would not accrue the kind of economic and non-economic benefits that a forum like APEC offers for a country like India which has targeted large-scale foreign investments and a manifold increase in its trade volume in the coming years. It needs no reiteration that, outside West Europe, most of the capital surplus nations are in the Asia Pacific. India desire to join APEC is a natural corollary to its new initiative of 'Look East policy' embarked upon in the early 1990s.

From the point of view of APEC it makes little sense to keep world's second largest country out of its ambit, particularly in view of the recent concerted moves by India to integrate itself with global economic dynamics more closely. World Bank has predicted that by 2020 India would be the fourth largest economy in the world and it is already one of the large emerging markets. One way to expedite India's economic reforms would be to admit it into APEC and make it conform to the collective decisions. Thus, a base for mutually beneficial relationship could be well laid between India and the rest of APEC countries. India is already a Dialogue Partner of ASEAN and a member of ASEAN's security forum, the ASEAN Regional Forum (ARF), which is a testimony to the fact that India as an important power could no longer be ignored. Also, a majority of the top investors in India in the last few years have been APEC member countries and these nations have already emerged as the most important trading partners of India.

Indian policymakers do not seem to have understood that APEC is as much a political forum as an economic one. Its political agenda became obvious when Russia was included. Each nation in APEC, especially the major ones, has a political objective and unless this is understood New Delhi would be groping in the dark. For instance, for Japan, APEC is a forum to underpin its economic interests with long-term political strategy, to demonstrate that it wants to pursue a larger political role commensurate with its economic strength through multilateral fora. Indian entry into APEC would depend on how far it has gone and is willing to go in further liberalising its trade and investment regimes. Although there was a wide divergence in the Individual Action Plans of APEC members, but most of them have far fewer barriers than India. India should have brought out an Action Plan of trade and investment liberalisation on its own a long time back by bringing down its barriers to the average level of APEC states and demonstrated its sincerity in further reducing these barriers in the coming years.

Among the five organisations, under discussion in this chapter two organisations i.e. BRICS (Chapter-V) and ASEAN (Chapter II) have been dealt with in other chapters in details. However, BRICS includes Brazil, Russia, India, China, South Africa i.e. the prominent emerging economies of the world.

Russia and India's Export toward different organisations

The following two Tables (3.4 and 3.5) two tables' highlight value of Russia's export to five organisations, India's export to five organisations and relative percentage in comparison with the world as well as the Compound Annual Growth Rate during 2001-16. Here five economic organisations have been taken in to consideration while doing comparison. They are ASEAN, BRICS, SAARC, EU and APEC. EU is the top export destination of Russia and APEC stands second position as per the table content.

Table 3.4: Russian Export to Various Organisations and World

Unit-Dollar in Thousand

YEAR	WORLD	ASEAN	BRICS	SAARC	EU	APEC
2001	99868397	1.20%	6.92%	1.26%	54.46%	15.14%
2002	106691998	1.42%	8.17%	1.66%	51.75%	15.27%
2003	133655685	1.13%	8.42%	2.17%	52.61%	14.51%
2004	181600379	0.98%	7.15%	1.59%	52.27%	14.84%
2005	241451657	0.89%	6.62%	1.18%	57.63%	12.42%
2006	301550666	0.65%	6.44%	1.19%	58.97%	11.88%
2007	352266399	0.73%	5.49%	1.03%	47.90%	11.53%
2008	467993955	0.93%	6.08%	1.31%	57.15%	12.99%
2009	301796059	1.20%	7.91%	2.20%	52.94%	14.95%
2010	397067521	1.64%	6.79%	1.59%	46.51%	16.41%
2011	516992618	1.64%	8.04%	1.15%	44.59%	17.39%
2012	524766421	1.39%	8.75%	1.74%	46.82%	17.43%
2013	527265919	1.61%	8.51%	1.59%	45.75%	18.84%
2014	497833529	2.37%	8.92%	1.07%	45.08%	21.02%
2015	343907652	1.56%	10.20%	1.57%	39.77%	21.89%
2016	285491052	1.95%	12.37%	2.27%	45.75%	23.63%
CAGR	9.7%	14.87%	12.62%	10.49%	7.8%	13.5%

Source: http://www.trademap.org/stDataSources.

Russia's export to the ASEAN relative to total exports to the world has increased from 1.20% in 2001 to 2.37% in 2014 and it has declined in recent years to 1.95% in 2016. The status of Russia's export to the SAARC in comparison with total export has increased from 1.26% in 2001 to 2.27% in 2016. The percentage of Russia's export to the BRICS in relation to total export has increased from 6.92% in 2001 to 12.37% in 2016.

Table 3.5: India's exports to various organisations during 2001-16

Unit-Thousand USD

Total export to YEAR	WORLD	ASEAN	BRICS	SAARC	EU	APEC
2001	**43878489**	9.0%	5.3%	4.8%	23.6%	44.7%
2002	**50097958**	7.6%	6.2%	4.8%	22.6%	47.8%
2003	**59360659**	8.5%	6.9%	6.5%	22.8%	46.3%
2004	**75904200**	9.9%	8.1%	6.0%	22.1%	44.9%
2005	**100352637**	10.2%	10.2%	5.4%	22.6%	40.0%
2006	**121200606**	10.2%	10.1%	5.1%	21.4%	44.0%
2007	**145898053**	9.5%	9.9%	5.4%	21.7%	41.5%
2008	**181860898**	10.7%	9.3%	5.6%	21.6%	39.7%
2009	**176765036**	10.1%	8.5%	4.2%	20.6%	38.1%
2010	**220408496**	10.4%	11.9%	5.0%	18.9%	40.9%
2011	**301483250**	11.4%	9.4%	4.3%	18.2%	39.2%
2012	**289564769**	11.2%	9.7%	4.7%	16.8%	41.0%
2013	**336611389**	11.3%	9.1%	5.0%	16.7%	39.9%
2014	**317544642**	9.9%	9.0%	6.2%	16.2%	39.1%
2015	**264381004**	10.0%	6.8%	6.5%	16.9%	41.0%
2016	**260326912**	10.1%	6.3%	6.5%	17.6%	42.3%
CAGR	**14.71**	16.39	15.97	15.42	11.75	13.5

Source: http://www.trademap.org/stDataSources.

ASEAN is in third position in the context of India though it is a young organisation. The percentage in the bracket shows the relative share of exports to each organisation as a proportion of total exports to the world to reflect the significance of each organisation as a trade partner of India.

The percentage of India's export to the ASEAN in relations to total export has increased from 9.0% in 2001 to 11.4% in 2011 and it has declined in recent years to 10.1% in 2016.

The percentage of India's export to the BRICS in relation to total export has increased from 5.3% in 2001 to 11.9% in 2010 and it has declined in recent years to 6.3%. The latest trading status of India with ASEAN is better vis-à-vis its status with BRICS. The percentage of India's export to the SAARC in comparison to total export has increased from 4.8% in 2001 to 6.5% in recent years in 2016 in spite of the unstable export rate. The percentage of Russia's export to the APEC in relation to total export has increased from 15.16% in 2001 to 23.63% in 2016. It is clear that APEC as export destination of Russia played significant role in comparison with other organisations. APEC is the top export destination of India. The export value of APEC was 44.7% in 2001 and come down 42.3% in 2016.

The proportion of Russia's export to the EU relative to total export has increased from 54.46% in 2001 to 58.97% in 2006 and it has declined in recent years to 45.75% in 2016. EU is first export destination of Russia in comparison to above five regional organisations but in the context of India, EU is the second. India's export value to EU was 23.6% in 2001 and it has gone up to 17.6% in recent years in 2016.

Compound Annual Growth Rate (CAGR)

Compound growth rates are calculated to show the growth of exports to different regional organisations during the study period. It is to be noted that since only five organisations have been selected for study in terms of exports from India the total percentage does not necessarily come to cent percent. Both the Table 3.3 and 3.4 reflect Compound Annual Growth Rate (CAGR) of exports of Russia and India to five organisations. The CAGR of Russia's export to ASEAN is 14.87%, which is maximum in comparison with other groups as well as exports to world. The CAGR of Russia with world is 9.7%. Russia is a minor player in Southeast Asia in comparison to other economic organisations and apart from natural resources, energy technology and arms sales, there seems scope for expansion in Russia-ASEAN trade. After the Sochi summit in 2016 hopefully Russia and ASEAN economic relation is under change towards more positive dynamics. The CAGR of India's export to ASEAN is 16.39% which is maximum in comparison with other groups as well as with that to the world. In terms of value of exports APEC and EU are found more significant export destinations of India whereas ASEAN occupies the third position followed by BRICS and SAARC. But exports to ASEAN has experienced highest growth rate during the study period. From the Table III it can be observed that the growth rate of ASEAN in comparison to other economic organisations has immense export scope for future.

Changing Personality Dimensions of Putin and Impact on Trade Fluctuation

Russia's export and import with world and ASEAN reveal that in 2010 it reached the maximum in terms of export to ASEAN i.e. 1.64% during the period from 2001-10. The soaring oil prices accounted for that. Putin showed his mettle as economic reformer in 2014 its displayed still better performance. Since it touched 2.37% marks. But again the oil price collapse impacted it in adverse way. In 2015 and 2016 it went down. One year a bit lower (1.95%) than that of 2014 and other years still further lower (1.56%). But the imports from ASEAN in these two years were higher than that of the year 2014. Russia restrained spending to reduce its deficit. It made attempts to check inflation. (Sharma, 2018) The Russian economy is set to recover from a bout of recession that started around 2014.

Personality, a psychological phenomenon, refers to those traits which distinguish an individual from others. It is not the observable behaviour of the individual as his dispositions that lie beneath his behaviour. Guilford defined personality as an individual's unique pattern of trait. Traits are distinguishable relatively enduring way in which one individual differs from others.(Guilford,1959) The leader is a product of the environment and he also leaves his imprint on it. The likelihood of his impact on event or a policy varies with the personal strength and weakness of the actor. (Greenstein,1972) Putin who emerged as a charismatic leader and a strong personality on the Russian scene has undergone different phrases of his personality evolution i.e. as an economic reformer, as a nationalist a cautious economic decision-maker and aggressively provocative abroad. Putin has successfully projected himself as a strong leader who could restore Russia to its former glory. His macho image has been a salve for though who were left distraught by the collapse of the Soviet Union. (TOI, 2018)

Putin the economic reformer during the first decade of his tenure gave way to Putin the nationalist subsequently. He dispatched disguised soldiers to attack Ukraine and declared proudly about a missile capable of piercing air defences like a meteorite. (Sharma, 2018) He succeeded in wresting Crimea from Ukraine.

Summary

Russia's interest in Southeast Asia is considered as an indicator of the new system of world order. At present Russia is no longer considered a threat by ASEAN. Southeast Asia was generally neglected in Russian foreign policy during the Yeltsin years (1991–99), ASEAN's importance for Russia grew because of its expanded membership and leading role in East Asian regionalism. Russia under Putin attached greater importance to relations with Asia more generally and has tried to position itself as a significant regional player. Moscow sees ASEAN as ripe with opportunities for Russia to enhance its influence in Southeast Asia. This chapter focused on resurgent Russia's political and economic interests in Southeast Asia, which need to be emphasised. The changing environment of world politics is looking for expansion of the new connection of Russian Federation and SEA nations. Members of SEA region have established trade relations with Russia to boost their economic relation. Vietnam is the most befitting example. SEA nations purchased defence product from Russia's revitalised defence industry. It is important to have a clear understanding of the economic ties that bring them together. It is pointed out that Russia's import from ASEAN has grown impressively in comparison of Russia's export to ASEAN during 2001-16. One hypothesis that the resurgence of Russia helps the country to develop more interest in SEA stands vindicated. This chapter's prime focus is on Putin's politics and how his personality impacted the economy. Increasingly under Putin, Russia attempted to use its energy and military resources to project its influence into Southeast Asia. At present it wants to diversify away from oil and guns.

Chapter - IV

Indo-Russia Cooperation in SEA

Russia has been a pillar of strength at difficult moments in India's history. Russia is dedicated to promote strengthening its special privileged partnership with the Republic of India based on the convergence of foreign policy priorities, historical friendship and deep mutual trust, as well as enhancing mutually beneficial bilateral ties in all areas, primarily in trade and economy, with a focus on implementing long-term cooperation programmes approved by the two countries. India and the resurgent Russia have acquired a new self-confidence arising out of their rapid economic growth and expanding political cooperation. India-Russia relationship is one of deep friendship and mutual confidence that would not be affected by transient political trends. India-Russia relation remains vital for both countries amid a changing regional and global security environment. By all accounts Indo-Russia Cooperation in South East Asia region leads to achieve the strategic interest in the changing international scenario. In some context India played an important role in making a potential bridge between Russia and ASEAN. This chapter sets out to trace the changing contour in India's role to create strategic cooperation of Indo-Russia jointly with SEA Region. Both India and Russia jointly have planned to explore ASEAN as alternative venue. It needs to be reiterated that during the period of globalisation ASEAN has achieved considerable prosperity.

INDO-RUSSIA COOPERATION IN SEA

Russia has been historically the most important partner of India.

As discussed in the first chapter, India-Russia relationship always moves on abiding friendship and mutual trust. As rising economic powers, both India and Russia are playing increasingly larger roles on the world stage. India and Russia are engaged in several multilateral efforts such as the BRICS and the Shanghai Cooperation Organisation. Both are agreed to strengthen the defence partnership in line with the "Make in India" programme. India's focus on a strengthened and multi-faceted relationship with ASEAN is an outcome of the significant changes in the world's political and economic scenario. Prof. Chenoy examining how both India and Russia had contributed towards multipolarity in the current global system, elaborated on the dual aspects of multipolarity i.e. multilateralism and global governance, stating that both countries had a common understanding of the same. While outlining the importance of multilateralism in the current global architecture, she emphasised the role played by multilateral organisations, using the example of BRICS, where both India and Russia are involved. She also mentioned how no other international forum had developed institutions like BRICS had, and asserted the importance of other regional organisations such as ASEAN. (ORF, 2018) In the globalisation era SEA Nations are emerging as economic powers and the importance of ASEAN is also increasing as an economic organisation. During leadership of Putin, cooperation with regional organisation is given more importance.

Responding to a question on Indo-Russia cooperation in South East Asia a diplomat viewed that what matters in foreign policy is based on national interest and as long as both India and Russia see benefit for their respective national interests, they will continue to cooperate and invent new areas of cooperation. Both the countries are drawn towards SEA/ASEAN to enhance their trade prospects. Attempt has been made to find out if there any cooperation in their trade relations with ASEAN. The thrust of the thesis is on the trend in this drive facilitating the emergence of a multipolar world. As mentioned earlier this cooperation is possible since there is no more suspicion by SEA nations towards Indo-Russia relation. In this context one question has been asked to the diplomat respondents **"Is there any suspicion continuing with some countries of SEA towards India and Russia as before?"**

The consensus among the respondents is that there is no longer any reason for the intense political suspicion and fear that characterised the relationship between Soviet Russia with India during the period of cold war when SEA was one of the most violent and bitterly contested zones of international rivalry. In this context one of the diplomats answered that in the new age of globalised relations and multilateral diplomacy, with lack of enduring ideological effects in the SEA region, no country can afford to nurse suspicion, more so towards India which has offered a hand of friendship and cooperation on equal terms. This goes back to Nehruvian times when India projected itself as a leader supporting liberation movements in the region. As regards Russia, it was tainted in the past in ideological colours. But with the fall and break-up of the Soviet Union in the early 1990s, Russia had to come to terms with a changed world, particularly with ASEAN having taken centre stage in regional multilateralism.

The broad area of Indo-Russian cooperation is in the sphere of politics, economy, defence. However, in recent years economics has grown in importance with whole world. In the context of Indo-Russia cooperation in SEA has been given special focus on economic, political as well as defence cooperation.

POLITICAL COOPERATION

Political cooperation broadly denotes working together of governments of differing states towards a common goal. This cooperation can occur in areas like military alliances and the settlement of territorial boundaries etc. Political cooperation between the two friendly countries has been historic from Soviet support in International forum on the issue of Kashmir to the signing of Indo-Soviet friendship treaty on the eve of Bangladesh war. In the moment of international crisis Soviet Russia stood firmly by India. Even in the Chinese invasion in 1962, though both China and Soviet Russia belonged to communist fraternity, yet Soviet Russia first remained neutral and then supported India. It there by saved Indian policy of non-alignment pursued under the leadership of Nehru from embarrassment.(Acharya,1992) This political cooperation is enhanced in the relation between India and Russia in the arena of terrorism.

TERRORISM AND THE SPILL-OVER EFFECTS

An unprecedented fluidity has crept into international politics because of emergence of the specter of terrorism. Thus, terrorism may be state sponsored or by non-state actors. Sometime it may be by both. International terrorism has assumed a menacing proportion. Because of the threat perception that nuclear weapons may fall in to the hands of terrorists, especially in a country like Pakistan, has created further complication. The democratic countries and not the effective dictatorships are more victims of terrorism. India and US the two largest democracies have to bear the brunt of Islamic terrorism. (Acharya, 2015) In fact, in the light of terrorist menace haunting the western world and country like Afghanistan and India, nobody knows who can do what to whom and when. The emergence of international terrorism as a big menace and the new and strong commitment of the international community to wipe it out came to be a new reality of international relations. The non-state actors have come to play a bigger role in shaping international relations. Russia and India both face the problem of terrorism and the spill-over effects from regional conflicts. They share an understanding of the cause and source of terrorism. (Chenoy, 2010) The tenth meeting of the Russian-Indian working group on combating international terrorism was presided over by the deputy foreign ministers of both countries in 2018. They reaffirmed their firm stand on the need to consolidate the efforts of the international community, led and coordinated by the UN, in the global fight against international terrorism and extremism based on the norms and principles of international law without any double standards. The parties assessed the state of terrorist threats in various regions of the world, including the Middle East, Afghanistan and South, Southeast and Central Asia. This shows that both the parties are seized of the problem of terrorism not only in South Asia but also in South East Asia. Russia and India also held high-level consultations on counter terrorism issues in New Delhi on Jan. 31, 2017. Both sides shared views and assessment on the threats posed by the scourge of terrorism, including state-sponsored, cross-border terrorism faced by India. Delhi Declaration issued following Summit held on 25th January, 2018 and focused both India and the 10-nation Association of Southeast Asian Nations agreeing to "deepen cooperation in combating terrorism in all its forms and manifestations, violent extremism and radicalisation through information sharing, law enforcement cooperation and capacity building under the existing ASEAN-led mechanisms". (Business standard, 2018) Stating that India's Act East policy reinforces its ancient links with Southeast Asia through enhanced political, security, economic and cultural ties, Kovind said: "In this context, India greatly values Asean's role as a proponent of peace, stability and prosperity in the region. (Business Standard, 2018) The 2001 ASEAN Declaration on Joint Action to Counter Terrorism, the 2004 ASEAN – Russian Federation Joint Declaration for Cooperation to Combat International Terrorism, the 2007 ASEAN Convention on Counter Terrorism, The ASEAN Comprehensive Plan of Action on Counter Terrorism, the 2016 Sochi Declaration of the ASEAN – Russian Federation Commemorative Summit to mark the 20th Anniversary of ASEAN – Russian Federation Dialogue Partnership "Moving Towards a Strategic Partnership for Mutual Benefit", the Comprehensive Plan of Action to Promote Cooperation between the Association of the Southeast Asia Nations and the Russian Federation (2016-2020) are steps in that direction. A joint statement after PM Modi's meeting with Russian President Putin "noted the commonality of positions of both the countries on such issues as war on terrorism. Indian side expressed its appreciation for Russia's unequivocal condemnation of the terrorist attack on army base in Uri." PM Modi said, "An old friend is better than two new friends." Both the leaders expressed their zero tolerance towards terrorism. Prime Minister Narendra Modi held separate bilateral meetings with the leaders of the two countries – ahead of Sunday's BRICS Summit – focusing most of his discussions on the need for countries to deny sanctuaries to terrorists and reconsider the way the United Nations designates terrorists. While Russian President Vladimir Putin strongly condemned terrorism in all forms, prompting Modi to say Moscow's stand on the issue "mirrors our own", Indian officials speaking about the prime minister's meeting with Chinese President Xi Jinping used rather defensive language, signaling little progress in those talks. Beijing gave no assurance on supporting New Delhi's bid on a UN ban against Pakistan-based militant leader Masood

Azhar, saying no more than that terrorism was a "key issue" and the two sides should strengthen their security dialogue and partnership.

A trend is discernible India and ASEAN have made joint declaration condemning terrorism. Russia has consistently denounced the offence. Initially, even USA used to take recourse to double speaks on the issue of terrorism and does not waver on it any longer. This not only assuages the feelings of India which has been the worst victim of terrorism it also gets partners in its much needed fight against international terrorism.

India has bilateral arrangements with several countries including Vietnam which impact security matters. India has been an active participant in the Regional Cooperation Agreement on combating piracy and Armed Robbery against ships in Asia. Indian decision makers started attaching top priority to maritime security after the terrorists of 26/11 hijacked an Indian ship and could reach the shores of Mumbai. The region's increasing headache about Islamic fundamentalism after the Bali bombings gets reflection in the counter-terrorism agreement with ASEAN. Joint naval exercises with Singapore since 1993, with Indonesia since 2002 and occasionally, since 2000, with Vietnam are steps in that direction. Some exercises have involved Malaysia, Thailand and the Philippines. Even one such exercises featuring India, Singapore, Japan and Australia is enough to send terror down the spine of China. (Tharoor, 2012)

ECONOMIC RELATION

Though political relations continue to determine the course of international relations yet international economic relations have gained tremendous importance. Conduct of economic relations is now regarded even more important than political relations among nations. This trend towards institutionalisation of relations and regional/global integration is a welcome trend since it is based upon the principle of mutual benefits through organised mutual efforts. Globalisation reflects the new urge for international integration. It is well said that geopolitics in the age of globalisation has been transformed into geo-economics.

Here we can analyze the economic cooperation of India and Russia in South East Asia Nations.

TRADE BETWEEN INDIA, RUSSIA IN THE CONTEXT OF SEA RELATIONS

No-doubt Indo-Russian relationship is not narrowly confined to "buyer-seller relationship." Both countries are optimistic about their firm and durable relationship in political and strategic fields as well as in trade and also economic interactions. The most important factor that the changing world order has to contend with is the rise of Asia, specifically the rise of China. Russia's turning eastward towards India, China and the ASEAN countries has to be reckoned with. Aided considerably by anti-US feelings in the region - there were widespread anti-US protests before the Iraq war in several ASEAN nations.

AREAS OF TRADE RELATIONS

The Partner country of India i.e. Russia is among the largest export economies in the world. Russia's top exports included crude and refined petroleum, natural gas, coal, semi-finished iron, aluminum, wheat, gold, diamonds, and copper among others. The export sector has played a significant role in the economy of Russia. Russia's immense wealth of oil and mineral resources allow the country to export large quantities of petroleum, natural gas, and several mined minerals. Some sources estimate that Russia contains more than 30% of the natural resources in the world which are among the top export products in the world. The World Bank estimates that the total value of natural resources in Russia accounts for $75 trillion. Since the country has an abundance of oil, natural gas, and precious metals such gold and aluminum, they account for a significant share of Russia's exports. Major items of export from India include pharmaceuticals; tea, coffee and tobacco; nuclear reactors and boilers; machinery and mechanical appliances; organic chemicals and electrical machinery and equipment. Major items of import from Russia include pearls, precious and semi-precious stones and metals; nuclear power equipment; electrical machinery and equipment; mineral, oil and its products; iron and steels; optical, precision and surgical equipment. Russian firms have shown a willingness to invest in India in construction, major infrastructure projects such as dedicated freight corridors and industrial clusters, smart cities, and engineering services, sharing technologies and skills. Indian companies are exploring major investment options in Russia, especially in natural resources such as coal, fertilisers, hydrocarbons, minerals, and rare earth metals. (The Indian Express, 2017) It should be focused that among South East Asian region Singapore, Vietnam, Malyasia, Indonesia and Thailand are the export destinations from India's top 25 export destinations according to the data of India's Trade Portal. It has mentioned in the Chapter-II as quantitative figure (Table 2.2). It is important for great powers like India and Russia to maximize the "arc of advantage" by strengthening relationships with South East Asian countries.

On the other hand, Vietnam and Indonesia purchase a significant proportion of their total military hardware from Russia. But if we take year-wise account in terms of exports to the ASEAN countries, we find Vietnam has received more vis-à-vis Singapore in particular years. Russian exports play a much smaller role in Burma, Malaysia, and Thailand still the higher growth rate gives positive sign for present Myanmar and Thailand. Russian defence manufacturers have not sold any weapons to Philippines, Singapore but total exports of Russia to Singapore and Philippines is moderate. So it can be said that there is lot of future prospect of trade relation among Russia and SEA nations. Although India initiated tentative defence engagement with Southeast Asian nations from the early 1990s, it was the conclusion of a bilateral defence cooperation agreement with Singapore in 2003 that launched vigorous security diplomacy in the region.

DEFENCE COOPERATION OF INDIA-RUSSIA IN THE CONTEXT OF SEA

Indo-Russia bilateral ties have traditionally been very close and Russia has been a long-standing defence partner of India. Their defence ties got a new impetus under the dispensation of President Vladimir Putin. In this connection Jaitley said "Here again, Russia as India's largest, oldest and most trusted partner in defence hardware and equipment, would have a comparative advantage in partnering with Indian companies for realising 'Make in India' potential in defence production,", according to the Press Trust of India. Russian-Indian cooperation remains supreme in the defence sector. Russia has undeniably sold India some weapons systems that it offers no other foreign clients. These sales and other defence cooperation have been institutionalised in usual meetings of the Russian-Indian Governmental Commission on Military Technical Cooperation, which meets annually at the level of Defence Ministers. Russia is the only country with which India has such an institutionalised military cooperation mechanism at such a high level. Generally, India still purchases most advanced military systems from foreign suppliers, especially Russian companies. Some two-thirds of India's defence procurement budget is spent on foreign-supplied weapons and services, making India the largest arms importer in the world. (Amit, 2011) Russia has sought to meet Indian demands that Russia transfer more defence technologies to India and, in line with Moscow's increased willingness to import weapons and co-produce them, engage with India in more joint research, development, and production of new military systems.

Though of late, USA has emerged as the largest supplier to India in the field of defence. Yet it is basically selling defensive system to India like the P-8I maritime surveillance aircraft and the C-17 Globe-Master III and C-130J Super Hercules military transport planes. Russia on the contrary has transferred offensive weapon system to India, including strategic bombers Sukhoi-30MKI an aircraft carrier (INS Vikramaditya) convention submarines and a nuclear powered submarine (INS Chakra). Russia is only foreign power helping India with strategic projects like the Arihant nuclear submarine. It is willing to sell India the lethal, interceptor based S-400 Triumf air defence system and also lease a second nuclear powered submarine. (Chellaney, 2018) HAL is a symbol of Indo-Russian cooperation that too in the context of South East Asia. HAL is a state owned company of India. Amalgamation of the two companies i.e. Hindustan Aircraft Limited and Aeronautics India Limited was brought about on 1st Oct 1964 by an Amalgamation order issued by the Government of India and the Company after the amalgamation was named as "Hindustan Aeronautics Limited (HAL)" with its principal business being design, development, manufacture, repair and overhaul of aircraft, helicopter, engines and related systems like avionics, instruments and accessories. Russian Aircraft Corporation MiG, Russia, Royal Malaysian Air Force, Malaysia, Royal Thai Airforce, Thailand, Rosoboronexport, Russia, Vietnam Airforce, Vietnam are the major international customers of HAL. State-run Hindustan Aeronautics Ltd (HAL) has joint venture 50-50% partnership with UAC-TA (United Aircraft Corporation-Transport Aircraft) and Rosoboron-export of Russia in respect of multi-role transport aircrafts design, development, manufacture, marketing and providing product support.

Joint Venture Companies are concerned with Overhaul and repair of aircraft, engines, aggregates and systems, Product support for maintenance and exploitation of aircraft, Production of aircrafts, engines, aggregates in India/Russia on the basis of Cooperation and supply of ground and role support equipment.

Russian Firms and Indian firms which constitute joint venture companies are constituted as follows:

RAC- MiG -	31%
Ryazan SIP -	10%
Aviazapchast Plc -	6%
Indian Firms ICICI Bank -	5%
HAL -	48%

With the signing of agreement with Russian partners to take up licence manufacture of Sukhoi 30 MKI Aircraft at the Nasik Division which had been engaged in manufacture and overhaul of MiG series Aircraft, had to be expanded. Accordingly it was decided in February, 2002 to have two Divisions at Nasik i.e. Aircraft Manufacturing Division for Su-30 MKI production and Aircraft Overhaul Division for overhaul and upgrade of existing MiG Series aircraft. Consequent on decision to manufacture AL 31 FP Engine for SU 30 MKI Aircraft, under licence from Russian Manufacturer, it was decided to establish a new Division at Koraput to take up the project in February, 2002. The project activities under the new Division have accordingly commenced. Russia and India are in the final stages of negotiations over the delivery date of new missile air defence systems and four *Admiral Grigorovich*-class frigates. Both sides also signed an agreement for India to lease an inactive *Akula* class multi-purpose nuclear submarine last year. Rosoboronexport, Russian Helicopters, and India's Hindustan Aeronautics Limited have also agreed to create a joint venture for the production of 140 Ka-226T helicopters in October 2016. (Gady, 2017) The tri-services exercise is being seen as a result of Prime Minister Narendra Modi's Russia visit in June when both countries had decided to "upgrade and intensify" defence cooperation through joint manufacture, co-production and co-development of key military hardware and equipment. (Baruah, 2018)

Asia is the most important foreign market for Russian arms producers, accounting for 70 percent of their exports since 2000. The major states are located in this area: India, China and Vietnam are the principal sources of demand for Russian weapons in the region, and Russia is the dominant supplier in a large proportion of Asian countries. Not only is Russia exporting a large volume of armaments across an increasingly wide range of product categories, it is also willing to sell the most technologically advanced equipment that in some cases is equivalent in capabilities to Western analogues, and that in other cases surpasses them. For instance, Russia has either agreed to sell, or is considering selling, the Su-35, an advanced 4++ generation fighter, to Indonesia; the extremely capable S-400 air-defence missile system to India; and Project 636M (Varshavyanka-class) diesel-electric attack submarines to Indonesia. It has also agreed to lease nuclear-powered attack submarines (SSNs) to India. (Connolly and Sendstad, 2017)

India and Russia signed billions of dollars' worth of military deals. The 16 agreements signed after the talks include three prominent deals on bilateral defence cooperation: Inter-Governmental Agreements (IGAs) for five S-400 'Triumph' air defence missile systems, four Admiral Grigorovich-class (Project 11356) guided missile stealth frigates and a share-holders agreement for a joint venture to manufacture 200 'Kamov'-226 helicopters in India. From 2012 to 2016, Russia supplied 68 percent of India's arms import, as per the survey by Stockholm International Peace Research Institute (SIPRI) – an international think-tank that researches on conflict, armaments, arms control and disarmament. In the same period, the US supplied 14 percent of arms to India, followed by Israel (7.2 percent). (The Indian Express, 2017) Due to the global flux underway US and Russia have started perceiving each other as strategic threat. India having good relations with both the powers is put in a disadvantageous position. The US state department's latest move on April 6 in notifying 39 Russian entities including the state owned arms exporter Rosoboronexport and warning that any significant transaction with these entities will entail US sanction has caused inconvenience for India. On the one hand US want India to be its closest strategic partner in Asia-Pacific as a hedge against China. On the other it is jeopardizing India's proposed acquisition of S-400 air defence missile systems from Russia as well as frigate submarine and helicopter projects. It will also reinforce suspicions in India about the US not being a reliable long term arms supplier. (TOI, 2018) External affairs minister Sushma Swaraj says "India follows only UN sanction not unilateral sanctions of any country". India has diplomatic space to rebuff US pressure because the US this time is acting alone with its own European allies. (Chellaney, 2018) India's capability to detect and destroy hostile fighters, strategic bombers, missiles and drones at long ranges will get a boost when a new squadron of the S-400 Triumf surface-to-air missile systems becomes operational along the northern borders with China shortly. (TOI, 2022)

India and Russia are therefore, working on a roadmap to get around the new US sanctions regime imposed by US congress through the CAATSA (Countering America's Adversaries through sanctions Act). In the latest informal summit meeting held between India and Russia, Modi told that the seed of partnership planted by Vajpayee and Putin in 2000 has grown in to a huge tree of privileged strategic partnership. Putin in his welcome remarks commented that a lot of momentum had been added to the bilateral relations in the strategic defence sphere. In the above background Indo-Russia special defence cooperation in South East region is getting boost. As mentioned above CAATSA sanctions are automatically imposed on countries acquiring weapons from some Russian state controls defence firm. However, given the fact that both defence secretary Jim Mattis and Secretary of state's Mike Pompeo have urged Congress to issue national security waivers and that both democrats and Republicans are concerned about winning over countries against China, there is a good chance that India, Indonesia and Vietnam will be granted waivers. (Chanda, 2018) ASEAN members have expressed interest in Russia's scientific technological potential and consider Russia as an attractive market for ASEAN investments, with its rich natural resources, and for traditional exports. Such circumstances provide a good opportunity for increasing investment flow to Russia from ASEAN countries and vice versa. It thus appears that relations between Russia and ASEAN have considerable potential for further development.

While discussing Indo-Russian cooperation in South East Asia, it can be pointed out that of trade in arms and weapons provides the thrust area. The Malaysian Air force in its search for modernisation ordered the purchase of 18 Su 30 MKMs in May 2003 after a close visit to see India's Su-30 MKI. It is to be noted that India and Russia being consistent friends have got partnership in the manufacture of weapons. The relationship stretches back over decades and during the cold war. India produced a range of Soviet weapons systems under licence including hundreds of MiG-21 and MiG 27 fighter aircraft. HAL is a witness to their collaboration in the production of different variants of Sukhoi. It is to be noted that Su 30 MKM was developed by the Sukhoi Design Bureau and is based on Su 30 MKI. Su 30 MKI in turn is derived from the Sukhoi. Su 27 MKM version differs from the MKI mainly in the composition of the on board avionics. It is further learnt that Irkut Corporation of Russia subcontracted the task of manufacturing the canards, stabilizers and fins to HAL. This shows intense collaboration between the two partners in defence production and which is sold in South East Asian Countries. It must be further noted that on 19th May 2007, Jamaluddin Jarjis, Malaysia's minister Science, Technology, innovation, announced that two Malaysian final candidates for astronauts would be undergoing training in Moscow as part of the billion dollar deal for 18 Sukhoi Su 30

MKM. Subsequently, an IAF training team was deployed in Malaysia to train Malaysian pilots on the Su-30 MKM aircraft from Feb 2008 to Sept. 2010 i.e. for two and half years. These involve Indian assistance in military training and arms transfers. India's arms exports are well below the level of Chinese volumes. India is already committed to servicing some Southeast Asian fighter aircraft purchased from Russia and training the military personnel from the region to operate them. India's expanding defence cooperation with Vietnam in particular has received special attention given New Delhi's past efforts at balancing Beijing in Indo-China. Some see it as the most consequential Indian strategic partnership in Asia.

In the spring and summer of 2007, the Indian Navy sailed all the way up to Vladivostok and conducted a series of bilateral and multilateral exercises with a number of nations that included major powers like the United States, Japan, Russia, and China as well as regional actors like Singapore, Vietnam, and the Philippines. India's military diplomacy in 2007 culminated in large-scale naval exercises with the United States, Japan, Australia, and Singapore in the Bay of Bengal. Beyond the expanded reach and scope of its recent external military engagement, India has stepped up its bilateral security cooperation across the region. During the last few years, India has signed security cooperation agreements with a number of Southeast Asian countries, including Singapore, Indonesia, Malaysia, Vietnam, and Cambodia.

In Feb. 2018, the Su-35 purchase contract was finalised by Indonesia. It would purchase II aircraft. By Oct. 2018 the first delivery is expected. India is found reluctant to order the Sukhoi/HAL/FGFA due to high cost and it has been reported that India and Russia are intending to upgrade the Su-35 with Stealth technology (similar to the F-15 silent Eagle) as an affordable alternative to the FGFA (Su-57). This clearly shows that India is acting as a gateway in the arms trade of Russia to the South East Asian countries.

Another important matter of cooperation is New Delhi has a comprehensive defence and security relationship with Vietnam. The growing number of high-level bilateral visits, annual security dialogues, and military-to-military cooperation are a sign of the growing convergence in security matters. The Joint Commission Meeting at the Foreign Ministers' level and the Foreign Office Consultations, Strategic Dialogue at the Foreign Secretary level, and Security Dialogue at the Defence Secretary level are some of the useful institutional mechanisms that have propelled the relationship. Beyond this and more important from the point of view of the present study is that India has been training the Vietnamese military in operating its Russian-built Kilo-class submarines and SU-30 fighter jets. This type of cooperation is also indicating the mutual cooperation of India and Russia in SEA nations. As noted earlier India is acting as a gateway in the arms trade of Russia to the South East Asian countries. Supply of military spares, maintenance of hardware, and ship visits are also other important facets of the defence cooperation. The two sides have also signed an MoU for Coast Guard-to-Coast Guard collaboration. During Prime Minister Modi's visit to Vietnam, New Delhi gave Hanoi a $500 million line of credit for defence cooperation. (Rajagopalan, 2018)

The MiG-29 has been a popular export aircraft. More than 30 nations either operate or have operated the aircraft to date, India being one of the largest export operators of the type. As of 2013, the MiG-29 is in production by Mikoyan, a subsidiary of United Aircraft Corporation (UAC) since 2006. The MiG-29's good operational record prompted India to sign a deal with Russia in 2005—2006 to upgrade all of its MiG-29s for US$888 million. Under the deal, the Indian MiGs were modified to be capable of deploying the R-77RVV-AE (AA-12 'Adder') air-to-air missile. The missiles had been tested with success in October 1998 and were integrated into IAF's MiG-29s. IAF has also granted the MiG Corporation another US$900 million contract to upgrade all of its 69 operational MiG-29s. These upgrades will include a new avionics kit, with the N-109 radar being replaced by a Phazotron *Zhuk-M* radar. The aircraft is also being equipped to enhance beyond-visual-range combat ability and for air-to-air refueling to increase endurance. In 2007, Russia also gave India's Hindustan Aeronautics Limited (HAL) a licence to manufacture 120 RD-33 series 3 turbofan engines for the upgrade. The upgrade will also include a new weapon control system, cockpit ergonomics, air-to-air missiles, high-accuracy air-to-ground missiles and "smart" aerial bombs. The first six MiG-29s will be upgraded in Russia while the remaining 63 MiGs will be upgraded at the HAL facility in India.

Another important thing is that Indian Air Force is planning to acquire the retiring Mig-29N of Malaysian Air Force. Indian Air Force is very keen to buy Malaysian Mig-29N as confirmed by the Malaysian Prime Minster Najib Razak. Indian Air Force has taken this step to stop the depleting fighter strength in the air force. It doesn't even have 70% of its fighters operational for any war like event. Indian Air Force is willing to share the spare parts of its Su-30MKI with Malaysia. Malaysia needs spares of Su-30Mki for its Su-30MKM. Malaysian Air Force in 2009 had quoted asking price of 300 Million Malaysian Ringgit for 16 Planes. That stood at 18.75 MR per Unit. It translates into 4$ Million a Unit for India if the price holds or India might also be able to fetch more discounts from Malaysia is yet to be seen. Myanmar was the last country to procure Legacy Mig-29 jets based on the original air frame design from Russia at around 31$ Million apiece. India was always perhaps the only country Malaysia was comfortable to sell the Fulcrums without any difficulty, among all other Mig-29 operators. India and Malaysia might agree for a Barter Type of Deal where the exchange of money might not happen and Malaysia might instead be paid back by the supply of spares for its Sukhoi-30MKM fleet.

In accordance with the agreement, Russia promised to deliver military hardware worth $3 billion, including the delivery of 320 T-90 Tanks, SU-30 aircraft, the Admiral Gorshkov aircraft-carrier (as a free gift) and MiG-29 fighter aircraft. On the eve of the signing of the Declaration on Strategic Partnership, Putin stated that it would "take our (Indo-Russian) political and defence cooperation back to the stage of the good old special relationship between the two countries. Our (New Delhi-Moscow) trade and economic cooperation (would) receive a strong footing in high-tech area."

All these goes to show that Russia is banking on export of its military Aircraft and other defence equipment. In this process India is playing the role of a partner especially in the context of South

East Asian market. Both India and Russia are finding ready markets in SEA countries like Malaysia, Indonesia, Myanmar, Vietnam. In the context of arms supplied to Vietnam it can be argued that Moscow's main interest lies in maintaining the bilateral relations and walking the line between two of its strategic partners i.e. China and Vietnam. The fact remains that Russia remains Vietnam's key arms trade partner, providing the very weapon systems that are raising the costs for a hypothetical Chinese attack. (Tsvetov, 2016) Russian weapons are still the hottest commodity on Southeast Asian markets. Again, Vietnam has historically been and still remains the region's largest buyer of Russian arms. Its significant acquisitions include fighter jets, frigates, anti-ship missiles, missile defence systems, and Varshavyanka submarines (the last of these submarines will be delivered to Vietnam in late 2016). Indonesia, Malaysia, Thailand, and Myanmar have also purchased Russian weapons, although in smaller quantities.

BRAHMOS AEROSPACE

The BrahMos is a joint venture between the Russian Federation's NPO Mashinostroeyenia and India's Defence Research and Development Organisation (DRDO) who together have formed BrahMos Aerospace. It is the fastest supersonic cruise missile in the world. BrahMos was the only cruise missile in the world that could be launched from land to land, land to ship, ship to ship, ship to land, submarine to land, submarine to ship, airplane to land, and airplane to ship.

The missile is named after two rivers, the Brahmaputra of India and the Moskva, Russia. The company was established with an authorised capital of $250 million with 50.5% from Indian side and 49.5% from Russian side. The company is responsible for designing, developing, producing and marketing the BRAHMOS supersonic cruise missile with active participation of a consortium of Indian and Russian industries. BrahMos Aerospace has said that several Southeast Asian and Latin American countries have expressed interest, with particular interest in Naval and coastal defense versions. These countries are Brunei, Indonesia, Malayasia, Vietnam, Venzuela, South Africa, Brazil.

At least five countries are interested in purchasing Russia and India's jointly developed BrahMos supersonic cruise missile. Reports last year, which were attributed to a BrahMos spokes person said that Malaysia, Indonesia and Vietnam were also interested in the missile. Of late Philipines signed an agreement of \$374.96 million on 28th January, 2022 between Brahmos Aerospace Private Ltd (BAPL) & Department of National Defence of the Republic of Philipines to procure shore based Antiship missile system by Philipines. This contract includes at least 3 batteries as part of the agreement. A battery will have at least 3 mobile firing units, plus attached command and control, radar and support vehicles and units. Each mobile firing unit has 3 ready to fire Brahmos antiship supersonic missiles, with the export variant having a maximum range of around 290 km. Thus it has become the first ASEAN member state to do so. Indonesia is also expected to go for a deal with India to import the Indo-Russian Brahmos supersonic cruise missile.

Hanoi has long relied on Russian-built planes, including roughly forty Su-30s. Notably, Indian pilots reportedly trained their Vietnamese counterparts to operate the Su-30s they purchased from Moscow. On May 12, 2022, India successfully launched the extended-range version of the BrahMos missile for the first time from Su-30MKI fighter aircraft. With this maiden launch, India will be able to carry out precision strikes against a land or sea target over a long range from Su-30MKI fighter aircraft. Hence the Su-30MKM was based on the Su-30MKI of the Indian Air Force, the extended-range version of the BrahMos missile is promote interest on ASEAN members. Both aircraft have common airframe, thrust vectoring engines and digital fly-by-wire system; however the MKM version differs from the MKI mainly in the composition of the onboard avionics.

Myanmar received its first batch of Su-30s from Russia, and could be another Southeast Asian nation interested in integrating the BrahMos cruise missile on these planes. It is commented that BrahMos is not only a successful joint venture but also a model for cooperation which has immense political value for the two countries.

The strength of the Russian economic presence besides defence equipment like aircraft in Southeast Asia lies in oil, gas and nuclear energy. Singapore and Malaysia currently buy Russian oil and Indonesia is also involved in several energy projects, but again it is Vietnam that is Russia's chief oil and gas importer, with projects in both Vietnam and Russia. The same is true of nuclear energy. Russia has nuclear power construction projects in Myanmar and Thailand, but its main project is building the Ninh Thuan-1 nuclear power plant in southern Vietnam, where it is also providing related services and training personnel. (Tsvetov, 2016)

OIL AND ENERGY SECTOR

Russia-India economic relationship is greatly dependent on collaboration between state-controlled companies. Recalling Russia's extended contribution in developing India's oil and gas sector beginning with the discovery of Mumbai high field in the 1970's the long term gas supply establishes an energy bride between the two countries.(Dutta, 2018) The state is a controlling shareholder in the majority of Russian companies cooperating with Indian partners, such as Rosneft, Novatek, Roscosmos, Rosatom, Rostech, or Schwabe. Rosneft takes the lead in Russia's petroleum industry and is the world's largest publicly traded petroleum company. Company's main activities include prospecting and exploration of hydrocarbon deposits, oil, gas and gas-condensate production, upstream offshore projects, processing, as well as oil, gas, and product marketing in Russia and abroad. Rosneft is prominent in oil refining in Russia. In connection with oil Rosneft while initiating business in India sees it as a starting point to expand in the Asia-Pacific region by supplying fuels to Indonesia, Vietnam, the Philippines and Australia. Among those Indonesia, Vietnam and Philippines are member states of ASEAN/ South East Asia. Rosneft's entry will change the market dynamics. (John, 2017) Rosneft is a global energy company with major assets located in Russia and a diversified portfolio in promising regions of international oil and gas sector, including Venezuela, Cuba, Canada, the USA, Brazil, Norway, Germany, Italy, Mongolia, Kyrgyzstan, China, Vietnam, Myanmar, Turkmenistan, Georgia, Armenia, Belarus, Ukraine, UAE, Egypt, Mozambique, Iraq and Indonesia.

Rosneft geography in Exploration and Production business segment encompasses all the key oil and gas regions of Russia, including Western and Eastern Siberia, Volga and Ural Regions, Far East, Timan-Pechora, Krasnodar Region and the shelf of Russian seas, including Arctic shelf, as well as promising regions abroad, including Latin America and South-Eastern Asia. Government-to-government interaction often leads to bureaucratic delays. There are difficulties in interaction between Russian public sector companies and Indian private companies. Obviously, both sides need to attract private sector companies, including start-ups to the business dialogue, and facilitate conditions for doing business. Finally, there is need to embrace new areas of economic relationship and, perhaps, digitalise the partnership to neutralise the geographical distance between the two countries. The acquisition of Essar Oil Ltd for nearly $13 billion by the Rosneft led consortium in August 2017 was the largest foreign direct investment (FDI) into the country till date and also the largest outbound investment from Russia. The deal will hopefully help the Russian company gain access to India's rising fuel market. India's oil refining capacity is set to jump 80%, or by 194 mt (mt), by 2030 as state refiners, Reliance Industries and Rosneft line up expansion plans, undeterred by the renewable explosion, hoping to meet future demand. RIL(NSE 2.15 %) plans to add 30 mt of refining capacity, a 50% increase, by 2030 and Essar Refinery, now controlled by Russian giant Rosneft, is targeting to more than double capacity by adding 25 mt by 2025, according to the unpublished oil ministry report. (Choudhary, 2018)

It is also necessary to take into account bilateral investment. In the last few years there has been an increase in investments from both sides. The acquisition of Essar Oil Ltd for nearly $13 billion by the Rosneft-led consortium in August 2017 was "the largest foreign direct investment (FDI) into the country till date and also the largest outbound investment from Russia". The deal will hopefully help the Russian company gain access to India's rising fuel market. India's investments in the Russian economy amount to over $8 billion and are mainly concentrated in the oil and gas and pharmaceutical sectors. Russian officialdom wants to fall into the same trap again, it should continue its pivot toward

Asia that seemingly has already taken place, and follow a multi-pronged Asian policy. This will enable Russia to have a real alternative to turn to, or at least an additional track, apart from its economic connections with Europe. In this light, developing a partnership with India as the leading power in South Asia, as well as building cooperation with Japan, South Korea and the ASEAN countries, is of highest significance for it. (Zakharov, 2017)

The diplomat respondents were asked to identify types of trade relations other than arms and oil that can flourish among India, Russia and members of ASEAN. One diplomat respondent specified other strategic commodities such as potash which is used for producing fertilisers. On being asked to identify factors that can create a strong bond between Russia and India towards SEA region, the same diplomat identified maritime connectivity and market integration of strategic commodities with India acting as a bridge between Russia and SEA. Another diplomat, however, while replying to the above second question relating to the strong bond between Russia and India in the context of SEA replied that this requires further investigation under a constantly evolving scenario. He added that China could be an elephant in the room in this equation. With its growing relations with Russia, unthinkable a decade before and distancing from India, examining the factors which could draw India and Russia together in to SEA has to take into account a host of imponderables. But he was candid enough in pointing out that this could land itself into an interesting study. He further added that each country in SEA will interact with India and Russia and vice-versa, as per its own national interests.

SUMMARY

In the context of changed global scenario after the end of cold war and the inauguration of globalisation of economy, it is commented that one super power emerged and the ideological umbilical cord uniting India and the then Soviet Russia was severed. But the fact remains that the two traditional partners continued their bonhomie. Both the countries are united against terrorism, the serpent under the grass. Russia is found unwavering and consistent in its support against terrorism. All the South East Asian countries are also unanimous in their condemnation of terrorism. Official declaration of ASEAN and India and Joint Indo-Russian declaration attest this fact. India which adopted LPG as its policy and the resurgent Russia carried on their friendship turned their attention to South East Asian markets and cooperated in carrying on their trade. Data from secondary sources and collected on the basis of interview of some respondent diplomats clearly shows that both these countries carried on their economic cooperation in the context of following defence items in SEA.

(i) Sukhoi 30

(ii) MiG

(iii) BrahMos (all defence equipment)

(iv) Roseneft-Essar (Oil)

Thus, India and Russia have been found to collaborate countries. India is found acting as the gateway for Russian trade with SEA in certain cases.

Chapter-V

Emergence of a multipolar world and Move in that direction

INTRODUCTION

Polarity in international relations is any of the various ways in which power is distributed within the international system. It describes the nature of the international system at any given period of time. One generally distinguishes four types of systems: unipolarity, bipolarity, tripolarity, and multipolarity for four or more centers of power. Unipolarity is used to describe the power structure when one superpower dominates alone. The end of the Cold War meant that the previous decades' superpower rivalry had ended. The days of cold war during which the super powers developed the capacity to destroy the world many times over and flexed their muscles against each other by changing regimes in client states are truly speaking behind us. Neither in geopolitics nor in economics is the world locked into the kinds of permanent and immutable coalitions of interest that marked the cold war. (Tharoor, 2012, p. 425) With the cold war drawing to its end, the United States surfaced as the sole dominating power in world politics as there were no real challengers to its hegemonic position. According to structural realists unipolarity is unstable because it progresses towards multipolarity, as other powers will seek to break the hegemony of the superpower. As Jean-Jacques Rousseau (1762) so eloquently put it: "The strongest is never enough to always be master." In 1990, Charles Krauthammer declared a "unipolar moment," arguing that "the center of world power is the unchallenged superpower, the United States." To many observers, the word "moment" (or "illusion") seemed an apt description of the durability of US hegemony. Today, many analysts believe that this neorealist prophecy is coming true and that unipolarity is coming to an end—even if the "moment" lasted longer than originally expected. The 2008 global financial crisis revealed cracks in the economic foundations of US hegemony, especially when compared to a number of more spritely "emerging economies." (Sears, 2016) A foreign policy based on the unipolar idea is bound to lead to military alliances, hegemonic policies and creation of regional hegemony that promotes regional tensions. This has been established recently in the occupation of Iraq and Afghanistan and is projected for Iran and Yemen. In the past Vietnam and several Latin American countries were part of this agenda. It is argued that the unipolar idea that was reinforced during the George W. Bush period in the US has been gently abandoned by the Obama administration. This argument is strengthened by the hit that the US has taken in the financial crises and the increased Chinese economic role in the US economy. (Chenoy, 2010)

MULTIPOLAR WORLD: A CONCEPTUAL ANALYSIS

Conceptually the 'Multipolar' world as opposed to the 'Unipolar' and 'bipolar' worlds is based on the creation of global norms for governance in terms of rights equality and democratic laws for the international system. In such an arrangement the global system does not rest with a single (Unipolar world) or a couple of significant nations (bipolar or tripolar world) but rather with numerous nations with varying capabilities. Multipolarity will go down in history as a justified intellectual and political reaction to the arrogance, haughtiness and excesses of the unipolar world.

It is suggested that classical multipolarity cannot have water tight compartments i.e. rigid divisions between those who are right and those who are wrong, between friends and foes. Foes may turn out to be friends, those in the right and those in the wrong may swap places. On the contrary in the bipolar scenario friends are always in the right and foes are invariably in the wrong. Friends are forgiven for their mistakes and the foes are not. It is criticized that the popular 'collective west' notion in Russia does not fit in with the declared multipolar picture of the world. But Andrey Kortunov the critic himself admits that Russian politics in the Middle East is an exception, since Trump administration has been caught there in the trap of a bipolar world view, but Russia has projected its image of a regional referee. Russia, it is criticized, has been less successful in the Russia-China-India triangle that Yevgeny Primakov had promoted as the foundation of a multipolar world. (Kortunov, 2018).

The two terms 'Multilateralism' and 'Multipolarity' sound similar. But in meaning they differ. 'Multipolarity' involves building a new world order on the basis of power while Multilateralism is based on interests. The privileges of leaders is consolidated by multipolarity where as additional opportunities are provided to the under achievers by Multilateralism. Finally a multipolar world is built from blocs that balance each other while a multilateral world is built from complementary regimes. European Union, BRICS and ASEAN are the manifestations of multilateralism.

The Multipolar Theory symbolises a unique direction that cannot be qualified simply in terms of "progress/conservatism", "old/new", "development/stagnation", etc. The unipolar and globalist view on history conceives of the historical process as a linear motion from the worse to the better, from the underdeveloped to the developed, and so on and so forth. In this context, globalisation is seen as the horizon of a universal future. The ascendancy of certain nations beyond the west is pivotal to the reshaping of the international system in the first quarter of the 21st century. The rise of these states has introduced some uneven characters in the international framework and at a time of globalisation which has mirrored the great impact of traditional strong states and commercial actors. (Roy, 2016) The picture of a multipolar world with an agreeable face is based on their interests springing out of evolving systemic relationship among states. Multipolarism is a look into the future (that which has not yet been), a project of organisation of the world order on absolutely new principles and elements, and thus, a serious revision of the ideological, philosophical, and sociological postulates that modernity rests upon. Multipolarism is oriented towards the construction of that which has never been before it, to the creative strain of free spirit, the philosophical search and the striving for building a better, fair, harmonious, and healthy society. What is different, however, is that the character of this society, its principles and values, and also the methods to build its foundation, are perceived in a radically different way when compared to the globalists' vision. Multipolarism views the future to be multiple, full of variety, differentiated, dissimilar, and preserving a wide palette of collective and individual self-identification choices.

In the Multipolar world, every state having its particular noticeable qualities will wield decisive influence in the limited arena of affairs pertaining to its region. The USA is fast losing global influence though it had viewed itself, after the end of the Cold War, as the new hegemon in a unipolar world. In Asia, China, is seen as a keen contender for the position of a hegemon. The European Union, in spite of its current crises, perceives itself as a global player; the Eurasian land mass is assuming a new shape; Brazil and India have joined in the game. The hegemons seem to have had their days in global relations and been succeeded by a multipolarity. This raises the question of how the new and the old powers are going to conduct their conflicts from now on. Will arms races and economic warfare continue to dominate international relations, is the question mark.

India and Russia support the emergence of a multipolar world based on sovereign equality of all states and harp on the recognition of legitimate security interests of all states expressing their determined opposition to the unilateral use or threat of force in violation of the UN charter and to intervene in the internal affairs of other states, including under the guise of humanitarian intervention. Both countries have issued a political declaration on global challenges and threats to world security and stability, under which both countries have agreed to coordinate their efforts and positions on host of regional and international issues of mutual concern. (Mohanty, 2017)

The realistic notion mentions the path where both the countries actually stand and also important as it correctly reflects economic aims and power progressions, such an approach, can help in boosting Russia to structure Russia's modernisation, so as to hitch Russia's development to India's economic growth. Specifically these India-Russia ties should not be counted by India's cooperation with the United States, as any gain in this other relationship, is for certain socio-economic and trade patterns, which is not Russia's loss. India and Russia both are committed to the vision of a "Multi-polar world", where the goal is modifying one's diplomatic, trade and defence objectives. (Kulkarni, 2018)

In the post 1990's phase of globalisation, the narrative of a unipolar moment in contemporary history was given a different direction in the concept of a 'multipolar world' that was developed by Russia, India and China all of whom had new found interest in geo-economics and felt excluded from the dominant concept of a 'unipolar world' controlled by the single super power, the USA. This conceptualisation of multipolarity was understood clearly and it started becoming an actuality with the founding of new multilateral organisations like the BRICS and new security groups like SCO (Chenoy, 2016) ASEAN as a regional forum is contributing in this direction at present.

RECENT DEVELOPMENTS IN THE GLOBAL SCENARIO

In the system of changing world where new powers and new grouping are rising, Russia-China relations will form a key component in determining the evolution of the balance of power in the world. Though ideological and other differences developed between the two countries in the late 1950s relations improved dramatically after the fall of the Soviet Union. In 1991 and 1994, the two countries signed border agreements to delimit the eastern and western sections of their borders, but some minor sectors remained unresolved. The Sino-Russian relationship, while currently falling short of a full-fledged strategic partnership, has the potential to develop into one and completely alter the balance of power not only in Asia, but also globally. They are also engaged in multilateral fora such as RIC, SCO, and BRICS, and see such an engagement as one way of strengthening a multipolar world in which they are key players as well as a platform to present an alternative view point to the Western-dominated global discourse. (Unnikrishnan & Purushothaman, 2015) In the beginning of the 21st century, there appeared several definite indications towards the re-emergence of polycentrism. Russia, China, European Union, India, Japan, EU, the G-15 and some others began playing a more vigorous role by accepting the objective of ensuring a multi-polar international structure. Most of the states declared their resolve to secure and maintain the multi-polar character of the international system. Putin flexing his muscle in the international arena in recent years wresting Criemea from Ukraine, military intervening in Syria and even allegedly tipping the scales in US presidential elections- the perception of a strong Russia has been maintained. (TOI, 2018)

Syrian Civil War

Lack of freedoms and economic woes drove resentment of the Syrian government, the harsh crackdown on protesters inflamed public anger. Foreign backing and open intervention have played a large role in Syria's civil war. Russia entered the conflict in 2015 and has been the Assad government's main ally since then. The US has repeatedly stated its opposition to the Assad government backed by Russia but has not involved itself as deeply. In September 2015, Russia launched a bombing campaign against what it referred to as "terrorist groups" in Syria, which included ISIL as well as anti-Assad rebel groups backed by the USA. Russia has also deployed military advisers to shore up Assad's defences. At the UN Security Council, Russia and China have repeatedly vetoed Western-backed resolutions on Syria.

Russia's goals included helping the Syrian government retake territory from various anti-government groups that are labeled by the US and its coalition as "moderate opposition", a broader geopolitical objective being to roll back US influence. Lavrov, Russia's foreign minister has accused the US of trying to divide Syria while ignoring international law by launching missiles into the country. Present Syria problem showing resistance offered by resurgent Russia and western characterisation of it as cold war psychology.

Ukraine revolution

The United States and the EU wanted to convince Putin to stop supporting those in eastern Ukraine who want to break up the country. The United States claimed to have proof that Russia supplied separatists that shot down a Malaysia Airlines commercial jet over eastern Ukraine on July 17, killing 298 people.

In response to the Ukrainian revolution in 2014, Russia annexed the strategically important Crimean peninsula and provided covert military support to pro-Russian separatist rebels in the eastern Donbass province of Ukraine. Russia's military support to the Syrian government targeted US backed rebel forces, along with *Islamic State of Iraq and Syria* (ISIS) militants. Both of these events clearly reveal Russia's commitment to hard balancing against the US.

India has multifaceted relation with both the countries. Russia and India have maintained a durable partnership for decades, and India is a major buyer of Russian weapons. They also share a long history, and their relations are based on goodwill and friendship from the immediate post independence period to present times. But India's relations with China have been rougher, complicated by unresolved border issues. It is recommended by analysis that Russia must use these assets to ease tensions and normalise relations in the China-India relations. (Sushentsov, 2018) One point worth mentioning have is that in the context of comparative estimate of Russia's relations with India and that with China it is well pointed out that in maintaining best of relations with India, there is a consensus among the elite in Russia. But with regard to better relations with China there is no unanimity of views or consensus among the elite in Russia itself. This was corroborated by Sergei Karaganov, Economic and Foreign policy adviser to Russian President Vladimir Putin in his interview to Times of India. (Q&A, TOI 2018) This justifies the significance of the study undertaken even in the latest international context.

ATTEMPT OF INDIA-CHINA-RUSSIA TO USHER IN A MULTI POLAR WORLD

Regional cooperation for development, economic integration

came to be the order of the present world to secure sustainable development, protection of environment, nuclear-nonproliferation, elimination of terrorism and protection of states of all came to be the Global objectives. To secure the multi-centric structure of international relations came to be recognised as the common goal. The world got changed, and is still rapidly changing. In June 2005, China, India and Russia decided to forge and develop a common understanding and approach towards problems like terrorism and the need for the protection of their strategic interests. With Russia not playing an active role, China could shield Pakistani terrorist not only at the UN Security Council but also at a multilateral summit on Indian soil. In doing so, as Chellaney said, China rode roughshod over Indian concerns and showed itself culpable in the killing of 26 Indian soldiers at Uri and Pathankot. During the Goa summit BRICS members condemned the recent several attacks, against some BRICS countries, including that in India. They strongly denounce terrorism in all its forms and manifestations and stressed that there can be no justification whatsoever for any acts of terrorism, whether based upon ideological, religious, political, racial, ethnic or any other reasons. They agreed to strengthen cooperation in combating international terrorism both at the bilateral level and at international fora. To address the threat of chemical and biological terrorism, they support and emphasize the need for launching multilateral negotiations on an international convention for the suppression of acts of chemical and biological terrorism, including at the Conference on Disarmament. In this context, they welcome India's offer to host a Conference in 2018 aimed at strengthening international resolve in facing the challenge of the (Weapon of mass destruction) WMD-Terrorism nexus. They call upon all nations to adopt a comprehensive approach in combating terrorism, which should include countering violent extremism as and when conducive to terrorism, radicalisation, recruitment, movement of terrorists including Foreign Terrorist Fighters, blocking sources of financing terrorism, including through organised crime by means of money-laundering, drug trafficking, criminal activities, dismantling terrorist bases, and countering misuse of the Internet including social media by terror entities through misuse of the latest Information and Communication

Technologies (ICTs). Successfully combating terrorism requires a holistic approach. All counter-terrorism measures should uphold international law and respect human rights. They acknowledge the recent meeting of the BRICS High Representatives on National Security and, in this context, welcome the setting up and the first meeting of the BRICS Joint Working Group on Counter-Terrorism on 14 September 2016 in New Delhi. Stressing UN's central role in coordinating multilateral approaches against terrorism, they urge all nations to undertake effective implementation of relevant UN Security Council Resolutions, and reaffirm their commitment on increasing the effectiveness of the UN counter terrorism framework. They call upon all nations to work together to expedite the adoption of the Comprehensive Convention on International Terrorism (CCIT) in the UN General Assembly without any further delay. They earnestly recall the responsibility of all States to prevent terrorist actions from their territories. They reaffirm the member nation's commitment to the FATF (*Financial Action Task Force)* International Standards on Combating Money Laundering and the Financing of Terrorism and Proliferation and call for swift, effective and universal implementation of FATF Consolidated Strategy on Combating Terrorist Financing, including effective implementation of its operational plan. We seek to intensify our cooperation in FATF and FATF-style regional bodies (FSRBs). (BRICS Summit, 2016)

India-China- Russia strategic triangle took root with the end of the Cold War when the US assumed the role of global cop. The idea of the triangle raised much hope to build a multi-polar world that would enable the creation of a just and fair international economic and political order. The end of the Cold War conferred primacy to economics than to politics, much enthusiasm arose about a common economic agenda. This augured well for the three great Asian powers, India, China and Russia which shared the common goal of economic reform and modernisation. Being located in a single geopolitical space, they thought of a bonding to promote prosperity, security and stability in the region. (Bhattacharya, 2004) The Ufa BRICS/SCO summits offer an occasion for these three countries to rethink the RIC mechanism in terms of strengthening the trilateral order. The emphasis of this emergent order will not only be on how to increase the space and influence of the three countries, but on how to check the Western dominance in global financial decision-making. To promote a Russia-India-China triangular order, the bilateral understanding among the three countries is undoubtedly important. Russia and China have improved their mutual understanding in the recent past. The USA 'pivot' to Asia (seen as being antagonistic to China) and the increased Western antagonism towards Russia has brought the two countries closer, but this relationship is yet to be stabilised fully. A great level of mistrust still exists between the two. Meanwhile, India-China relations are marked by a range of conflict, cooperation and competition elements. A greater India-China understanding for a non-Western order, addressing a range of regional and global financial matters, is a common forte that must bring these two economies together. Likewise, India-Russia relations must be upgraded from their common standing of being satisfying to each other. Given the traditional bonding and depth of India and the Soviet world, relations with Russia must merit the first choice for India. Russian analysts have noticed India as very important part in the multipolar world order that they hope to promote to balance the power of the United States and its European and Asian allies. Yet, just as Indian leaders have made clear their unwillingness to align with the United States against China, so are they determined to avoid siding with Moscow against Washington. (Chenoy, 2010) The revival of the Russian economy under Putin and the continued growth of the Chinese and Indian economies have renewed interest in cooperating together on economic issues through the new BRICS (Brazil-Russia-India-China-South Africa) bloc of emerging economic powers. But thus far, the BRICS have only achieved modest economic cooperation through joint declarations and summits, demonstrating little if any strategic coordination. (Weitz, 2012)

Though the latest trend is that India is coming closer to USA and in view of the terrorist onslaught on the two democracies it is good that they are coming together and that trend was witnessed during Manmohan Singh's Prime ministership with regard to cooperation in peaceful use of nuclear energy; 123 agreement. This agreement was reached upon by United States of America and the Republic of India in 2008 and is known as the US - India Civil Nuclear Agreement. The deal is considered of huge worldwide political significance as the terms of the deal add a new dimension to international non-proliferation efforts. The deal was first introduced in a joint statement released by then US President Bush and Indian Prime Minister Manmohan Singh in 2005 and the deal took more than three years to materialise which lifts a three decade US suspension on nuclear trade with India. (Mian, 2006) Yet Russia on its part must accept India on a pragmatic note that even though India has a strategic understanding with the USA, it is purely based on India's national interest, and not intended against Russia. In return, India must start appreciating Russia and its revival as a power in global politics. In recent past Russia, India, and China met for their fifteenth ministerial trilateral meeting in New Delhi. Russia was represented by Foreign Minister Sergei Lavrov, India by External Affairs Minister Sushma Swaraj, and China by Foreign Minister Wang Yi. They have expressed satis-faction with the outcome of the 15th trilateral Academic Conference held in India in January 2017 and welcome the 16th Trilateral Academic Conference to be held in Russia next year. They welcome the first edition of the visit of RIC Young diplomats hosted by China in January 2017 and agree to hold the second such interaction in India in 2018.

It is a trilateral grouping of Russia, India and China that has met annually since 2002. In recent years, it has functioned as complement to other frameworks involving three countries are world powers with significant interests. A trilateral mechanism exists among the three neighbours, Russia, China and India, in the form of the RIC forum. Russians have continuing the traditional 'special' relationship with India as a means to balance American hegemony included Communists, Russian nationalists, and analysts and policymakers adhering to a 'Eurasian' outlook. They continued to exert considerable influence on Russian foreign policy in the 1990s since Yeltsin felt pressured to adopt some of their policy preferences in order to not appear as a Western lackey. Their weight increased substantially after Yeltsin felt compelled to dismiss the pro-West Kozyrev and replace him with Yevgeni Primakov, an influential Soviet-era policy analyst who advocated a Eurasian policy. Primakov served as Foreign Minister from January 1996 until September 1998, and then was promoted to Prime Minister until 12 May 1999. Primakov sought to rebalance Russian foreign policy by focusing more on developing ties with the emerging powers of Eurasia, especially by establishing a 'strategic triangle' among China, India, and Russia. One source binding these three states together was shared concerns about Islamic terrorism. Russia faced a secessionist movement in Chechnya, a predominately Muslim territory within Russia, Indians felt threatened by Islamic militants in Kashmir, while the Chinese were alarmed by Uighur nationalism in Xinjiang. Russia joined with India and China in defending the primacy of the principles of state sovereignty and non-intervention by foreign actors in their respective separatist regions of Chechnya, Kashmir, and Taiwan. (Weitz, 2012)

RIC is basically a soft network that lacks the vigour to forge concrete understanding among the partners on key global issues. Each is committed to the creation of a multi-polar world order based on respect for international law, multilateralism, and collective decision-making. The three also have strong ties binding them, though these are somewhat uneven. India, for example, has close political relations with Russia but the momentum of bilateral trade is yet to pick up. Russia-India trade is still below $10 billion mark. These economic relations are looking up. By contrast, India-China trade is thriving, but the bilateral political relationship could be better.

The threat of 'strongest sanctions in history' might bring together countries like India, Russia and China to resist this latest American move. Their commitment to a multipolar world order is going to be severely tested and India's Prime Minister's visit to Moscow augurs well for emerging countries. The beginning of this century saw emerging major regional players like Russia, China and India feeling uncomfortable with the unipolar world order and unilateralism that was being pursued by America and its allies in the 1990s. One of the major outcomes of the failure of the US-led global order was the coming together of emerging powers in the form of a global organisation called BRICS. Since its first summit,

BRICS has reiterated its commitment to build a multipolar world order. It has been highly critical of the unilateral moves by Western powers to remove leaders of sovereign states. (Pattnaik, 2018)

LATEST SHIFTS IN INDO-US INDO-RUSSIAN RELATIONS

India–Russia strategic partnership moved in the direction of greater cooperation in every respect but remained under the shadow of the emerging Indo-US strategic partnership. India-Russia relationship needs to be viewed in the context of new geopolitical and geo-economic shifts that are unfolding in the regional and global system. The current international order is characterised by the rapid shifting of global power to Asia; marked by, among other things, increasingly assertive role of China; the perceived shift in the US policy; Brexit and its impact on the EU; Russia's "pivot to Asia" policy; the growing Sino-Russian partnership; and the emergence of a new strategic partnership between India and the US. An analysis of the contemporary phase of the India-Russia engagement clearly points out that every effort is being made to strengthen cooperation between the two countries. Both countries have a common position on global and regional issues. They remain engaged through many multilateral groupings like BRICS, G-20, SCO, RIC and others. Both Russians and Indians have now accepted the reality that the new pragmatic relationship away from the old romanticism of the Indo-Soviet era needs to be developed. It is also true that despite many challenges there is a great deal of potential in the two countries to take the relationship to the next level.

STATUS AND PERCEPTION OF INDIA

It is well said that the US wants a unipolar world and a multi-polar Asia, China wants a unipolar Asia and a multipolar world, while India wants a multipolar Asia and a multipolar world. (Thapliyal, 2010) There is near unanimity in our country that India should contribute to a well ordered peaceful and equitable world and to democratic sustainable development for all. These objectives, as Tharoor points out need to be pursued keeping in mind the 21st century developments the end of the cold war, the emergence of the information era, the ease of worldwide travel, the blurring of national boundaries by movements, networks, the advent of Islamic terrorism as a plan global force, the irresistible rise of China as an incipient superpower while retaining its political authoritarianism. (Tharoor, 2012)

The economic growth of India and its entrepreneurial dynamism which flourished during the period of globalisation have carved out a prestigious place for India. In *Artha Sastra*, written in 4th century B.C, Kautilya remarked 'material well being is supreme'. India's economic growth twenty five centuries later has given much needed credibility to the international profile of India. From the discussion in the present study on Look East turned Act East Policy, the pattern of trade relations with ASEAN and other organisations, the individual countries of SEA. Indo-Russian trade from 2001-16 one can assess the increasing economic strength of India.

India's bilateral trade with ASEAN as a whole increased from $5.6 billion in 1998 to $ 14.5 billion in 2004 and the upward trend is maintained. The 'Asian Tigers' were economic dynamics to be emulated to the maximum possible extent by India. India was trying to emerge from cold war constrictions within the Indian sub-continent to its natural geographic position commanding the northern Indian ocean and bridging the different regions of Asia. (Mansingh, 2013) India has assumed international importance and its future potential is highly estimated.

India is gaining international prominence at a time when the world has moved in to a multipolar phase. This, Tharoor calls post-superpower age. At present, one witnesses a world of many rising (and some risen) each with substantial capacity in its own region, strong enough not to be swayed back and forth by a hegemon. They cooperate with one another in a series of networked relationships including bilateral and multilateral strategic partnerships that overlap with one another rather than tied in permanent alliances or locked in either or antagonisms. There is little room for domination by any superpower in the new networked world. Relationships have become contingent and they overlap with others.

Friends and allies united in one cause might be irrelevant to another cause or might find themselves, on opposite sides.

Constructing multipolar world is the continued agenda of both India and Russia. Russia knows that India was instrumental in the construction of a multipolar world order. It has benefitted India and Russia not to speak of others like China. Against the background of shifting alliances which has been discussed above Russia is closely associated with China, just as India is with the USA. In the globalised world each country can have cross-cutting relations without harming the core interests of the other. Chenoy hence argues that the Russian relations with China and Indian relations with the US will not affect adversely India-Russia relations. Russia's perception is that India is still their most reliable ally. They have no anxiety about the move of India as they do about that of others. (Chenoy, 2016) India and Russia need to pursue their strategic and economic partnership actively in the direction of strengthening a democratic multipolar world.

SOUTH EAST ASIAN SCENARIO

It is well commented that China wants a multipolar world but a unipolar Asia. But India is all set to thwart its intentions of emerging as a sole leader of Asia. Look East is not just an end in itself for India. It has not only facilitated greater economic cooperation with a long neglected region but has genuinely symbolised India's return, better called arrival, in a part of the world gradually anxious about China's arrogant presence. The latter phase of LEP marked an extended definition of East, extending from Australia to East Asia with ASEAN at its core. A shift from trade to wider economic and security issues was also discernible simultaneously. Hence joint efforts with India were undertaken to protect the sea lanes and coordinate counter terrorism activities.

The SEA region has been traditionally cautious about Chinese move. India, on the other hand, offers the region the prospect of a democratic and non-menacing counter balance. India was bogged down in its own neighbourhood and dismissed as at best a continental power. Look East Policy succeeded in lifting India from that not so comfortable position and in adding feathers to its cap in matters like diplomatic dialogue, strategic and military cooperation besides trade. It helped that both sides of the equation underwent a shared colonial experience, had cultural affinities going back to antiquity and despite the estrangement of cold war years a striking lack of historical resentments to come between them. (Tharoor, 2012)

India is a model for the SEA countries. The excellence of its institutions of higher education like the famous Indian Institutes of Technology and Managements have bestowed on Indian reputation in human resource development. That makes the country a source of attraction not for developing SEA countries like Indonesia, Malaysia and Singapore. Indian IT sector is lauded by the SEA countries and is a selling point. India is also ready to offer technical assistance in such areas of democracy promotion as public adminis-tration and the conduct of free and fair election. (Tharoor, 2012)

Gone are the days when ASEAN during the cold war was looked upon as a surrogate of USA. In the post cold war period geopolitics has been transformed into geo-economics. In such a context India is interested in carrying on trade and establishing other relations with SEA countries. In some cases in collaboration with the traditional partner Russia, it is engaged in carrying on such activities. In the process it is thwarting the attempts of China to forge a unipolar Asia. In fact, India and Russia can be characterised as two real partners in establishing a multipolar world and multipolar Asia. The SEA nations are also wary of dominance of any external power over them. Hence, Indo-Russian cooperation is welcome for them at present.

Summary

To sum up during globalisation post the 1990's the narrative of a unipolar moment in contemporary history gave way to a networked multipolar world. Though this world is democratic and small nation-states can also play their role, yet the key players who developed this multipolar world are Russia, India and China. The growth of economies of China and India was impressive and this was matched by the re-emergence of Russian economy since

2000. The reclaiming of Crimea, military counter attack to uphold the Assad regime marked the recalcitrant attitude of Russia in perception of the US led west. Russia's close relations with China and India's present proximity to US will not harm India-Russian relation. Both have a common understanding of the specificities of terrorism. The South East Asian nations also take unambiguous stand on this. India, Russia and China have been benefitted by the emergence of the multipolarity. To maintain this India and Russia specifically have to make efforts in this direction. Their cooperation in SEA which is the theme of the present study gives sufficient hope in this regard.

Chapter - VI

Conclusion

The following observation has been made on the basis of the study conducted on Indo-Russia cooperation in South East Asia.

India's interest to strengthen multi-faceted relationship with ASEAN (Association of South East Asian Nations) is a consequence of the major changes in the world's political and economic scenario since the early 1990s. India's exports to the ASEAN in proportion to the world exports has increased from 7.6% in 2001 to 11.4% in 2011 and it has declined in recent years to 10.1% in 2016. India's imports from ASEAN in proportion to India's total imports from the world have increased from 8.6% in 2001 to 10.7% in 2016. The compound annual growth rate of exports to and imports from ASEAN have increased at 16.39% and 17.74% respectively and which is more than that of its trade relation with the world. The trade balance indicates India is having favourable trade balance with ASEAN. The size of the positive trade balance has increased over the study period with some fluctuations. The trend of exports and imports between India and ASEAN countries reflects increasing trade openness in the last fifteen years especially since 2009 when FTA was signed. It is observed that the growth of India's exports to Cambodia, Laos, Brunei and Myanmar, Vietnam also confirm that ASEAN on the whole has great trade potential and Indo-ASEAN trade has a lot of scope for future. The growth rate of Vietnam also proves this New Delhi's views on Vietnam as "a strong pillar" of its AEP (Act East Policy), whereas Vietnam supports the policy, but wants India to play a more active role in the region's affairs. The bilateral relations among India and all South East Asian nations have got importance. It is high-lighted the importance of Look East Policy for India during the period of globalisation. The trade and the other relations of India with Southeast Asia have increased manifold during the period of globalisation. India has made extensive progress in implementing the India-Myanmar-Thailand Trilateral Highway and the Kaladan Multimodal Project, issues related to increasing the maritime and air connectivity between ASEAN and India. It is also getting importance in Modi period as 3 'C'(commerce, culture, and connectivity).

A resurgent Russia is focusing attention on SEA also. In the 21st century Russia-ASEAN trade has grown at an impressive rate with exports growing at a rate of 14.87% and imports growing at 20.05%. Russia's trade relation in terms of exports and imports as a proportion of its trade with the world has not been very significant, varying between 0.65% 2006 to 1.95% 2016. In most of the period imports size has been more than exports. One finds that Russia's import from ASEAN has grown impressively which was 1.38% in 2001 and which touched 4.39% in 2016.The above figure proves positive trade relation between Russia and ASEAN because Russia's import from the ASEAN is higher than export to it. The important finding is that the CAGR of Russia's import from ASEAN is higher than export to it. Russia's growth rate in connection with import from ASEAN is 20.05% and export to ASEAN is 14.87%. Singapore is the first export destination in comparison to other ASEAN member nations during the period 2001-16. It is to be noted that in the context of India, Singapore is also the first export destination. Singapore is the nation with whom Russia has the highest percentage of exports of total exports to ASEAN countries followed by Malaysia, Vietnam, Indonesia, and Thailand.

Among the SEA nations Vietnam played an important role for both the partners, India and Russia. It is worth noting that Vietnam is cold war ally of Russia. Russia's export and import with world and ASEAN reveal that in 2010 it reached the maximum in terms of export to ASEAN i.e. 1.64% during the period from 2001-10.

The soaring oil prices accounted for that. Putin showed his mettle as economic reformer. In 2014 it displayed still better performance since it touched 2.37% marks. But again the oil price collapse impacted it in adverse way. In 2015 and 2016 it went down. One year a bit lower (1.95%) than that of 2014 and other years still further lower (1.56%). Putin took cautious fiscal measures. He wanted to check inflation. ASEAN is seen as a rising center of power in Asia. A solid relationship could provide a greater balance in Russia's Asia policy, bolstering the multipolarity that ensures continuing Russian influence in world affairs in the face of American predominance. The ASEAN market holds much potential for Russia to project influence through its primary economic assets-arms and energy and for further expansion and diversification of economic ties. Putin's move is accordingly directed to achieve the goal of diversifying away from arms and oil.

ASEAN is seen as a rising center of power in Asia. A solid relationship could provide a greater balance in Russia's Asia policy, bolstering the multipolarity that ensures continuing Russian influence in world affairs in the face of American predominance. The ASEAN market holds much potential for Russia to project influence through its primary economic assets-arms and energy and for further expansion and diversification of economic ties.

Indo-Russia cooperation in SEA i.e. the crux of the matter in the present study relates to economic, political as well as defence cooperation. Political cooperation is enhanced in the relation between India and Russia in the arena of counter terrorism. In 2018 the tenth Russian Indian working group on combating international terrorism has identified South Asia and South East Asia as the regions affected by menace. India and ASEAN have made joint declaration condemning terrorism. Russia has consistently denounced the offence. Russia and India held high-level consultations on counter terrorism issues in New Delhi on Jan. 31, 2017. Both sides shared views and assessment on the threats posed by the scourge of terrorism, including state-sponsored, cross-border terrorism faced by India. Delhi Declaration issued following Summit held on 25th January, 2018. It focused both India and the 10-nation Association of Southeast Asian Nations (ASEAN) agreeing to "deepen cooperation in combating terrorism in all its forms and manifestations, violent extremism and radicalisation through information sharing, law enforcement cooperation and capacity building under the existing ASEAN-led mechanisms". Vietnam and Indonesia purchase a significant proportion of their total military hardware from Russia. But if we take year-wise account in terms of exports to the ASEAN countries, we find Vietnam has received more vis-à-vis Singapore in particular years. Russian exports play a much smaller role in Burma, Malaysia, and Thailand. Still the higher growth rate gives positive sign for present Myanmar and Thailand.

HAL is a symbol of Indo-Russian cooperation that too in the context of South East Asia. HAL is a state owned company of India. Hindustan Aeronautics Limited (HAL) with its principal business being design, development, manufacture, repair and overhaul of aircraft, helicopter, engines and related systems like avionics, instruments and accessories. RAC MIG, Russia, Royal Malaysian Air Force, Malaysia, Royal Thai Airforce, Thailand, (Russian company) Rosoboron export, Russia, Vietnam Airforce, Vietnam are the major international customers of HAL. State-run Hindustan Aeronautics Ltd (HAL) has joint venture 50-50% partnership with UAC-TA and Rosoboron export of Russia in respect of multi-role transport aircrafts design, development, manufacture, marketing and providing product support.

There are two Divisions at Nasik i.e. Aircraft Manufacturing Division for Su-30 MKI production and Aircraft Overhaul Division for overhaul and upgrade of existing MiG Series aircraft. Rosoboron export, Russian Helicopters, and India's Hindustan Aeronautics Limited (HAL) have also agreed to create a joint venture for the production of 140 Ka-226T helicopters in October 2016. By this process Indo-Russia special defence cooperation in South East region is getting boost. In Indo-Russian cooperation in South East Asia, it can be pointed out that trade in arms and weapons provide the thrust area. Su 30 MKM was developed by the Sukhoi Design Bureau and is based on Su 30 MKI. Two Malaysian final candidates for astronauts would be undergoing training in Moscow as part of the billion dollar deal for 18 Sukhoi Su 30 MKM. Subsequently, an IAF training team was deployed in Malaysia to train Malaysian pilots on the Su-30 MKM aircraft from Feb 2008 to Sept. 2010 i.e. for two and half years. In Feb. 2018, the Su-35 purchase contract was finalised by Indonesia.

India has been training the Vietnamese military in operating its Russian-built Kilo-class submarines and SU-30 fighter jets. This type of cooperation is also indicating the mutual cooperation of Indo-Russia in SEA nations. As noted earlier India is acting as a gateway in the arms trade of Russia to the South East Asian countries. Indian Air Force is willing to share the spare parts of its Su-30Mki with Malaysia. Malaysia needs spares of Su-30Mki for its Su-30MKM. Russia is banking on export of its military Aircraft and other defence equipment. In this process India is playing the role of a partner especially in the context of South East Asian market. Both India and Russia are finding ready markets in SEA countries like Malaysia, Indonesia, Myanmar, Vietnam. Though the exports of Russia out weigh the imports to ASEAN, yet its exports to Singapore, Vietnam, and Myanmar are more than the imports. Russia and India's jointly developed supersonic cruise missile is BrahMos. Malaysia, Indonesia and Vietnam were also interested in procuring the missile as published in the report 2017. Hanoi has long relied on Russian-built planes, including roughly forty Su-30s. Myanmar also recently signed a contract to purchase Su-30s from Russia, and could be another Southeast Asian nation interested in integrating the BrahMos cruise missile on these planes.

Rosneft is a leader in oil refining in Russia. In connection with oil Rosneft sees the India business as a starting point to expand in the Asia-Pacific region by supplying fuels to Indonesia, Vietnam, the Philippines and Australia. Among those Indonesia, Vietnam and Philippines are member states of ASEAN/ South East Asia. Rosneft's entry will change the market dynamics. The acquisition of Essar Oil Ltd of India for nearly \$13 billion by the Rosneftled consortium in August 2017 was "the largest foreign direct investment (FDI) into the country till date and also the largest outbound investment from Russia". This is more than a commercial deal and intended to facilitate cooperation between the two political leaders.

SUGGESTIONS

- Russia and India need to jointly work for an international convention against terrorism and in the mean time appoint a commission to put in black and white the varieties and codes on terrorism.
- Both of them have to revitalise their earlier agreement on sharing intelligence for a joint strategy to tackle the problem of terrorism.
- Russia India and South East Asian countries should have a greater say in global economic governance specifically the World Bank and IMF where their voice is not given importance.
- Indo-Russian trade itself needs to pick up momentum.
- Privatisation process needs to be expedited in both Russia and India because 70% of Russian economy still is under state control.
- No private company of Russia is among top hundred companies in the world. Hence if they want to cooperate more in the context of SEA market they have to further liberalise their economies.
- To retain a multipolar world both India and Russia need to be active strategic and economic allies.

CONCLUSION

India has historic cultural, religious, economic ties with the countries of South East Asia. Odisha's annual festival of 'Bali Jatra' symbolises the adventures of innumerable traders in pursuit of trade and culture. During the hey days of cold war, however, the relation of India and SEA did not blossom due to preoccupation of India with Pakistan factor and East-West rivalry. Indo-Soviet friendship used to be viewed with suspicion by most nations of SEA. But after the breakup of former USSR, the end of cold war and with the ushering in of liberalisation-privatisation and globalisation, the traditional Look East Policy revived. The prosperity of a significant number of South East Asian nations held out prospects for economically not so well off India at that point of time. Under the leadership of Narashima Rao and Manmohan Singh, the relationship between India and South East Asia got proper environment to blossom. Most of the countries of South East Asia appreciate India as upholding a strong democratic ethos and a benign foreign policy of mutual co-existence. India's export to the ASEAN in proportion to the world exports, as revealed by data, has grown from 7.6% in 2001 to 11.4% in 2011. The imports from ASEAN in proportion to India's total imports from the world have increased from 8.6% in 2001 to 10.7% in 2016. The increase is very significant since 2009 when FTA was signed between India and South East Asian countries. Giant steps are taken to provide communication facilities through land, water and air to facilitate trade and commerce with SEA. India and Nations of South East Asia have expressed common concern over the upsurge of terrorism especially after Bali bombings. Joint naval exercises are conducted by India and countries of SEA region like Indonesia, Singapore and Vietnam in this direction. Thus, there is no iota of doubt that the trade and other relations of India with South East Asia have increased manifold during globalisation.

So far as Indo-Russia friendship is concerned, it can be characterised as unique in the arena of International relations. Within the framework of non-alignment it cultivated special relationship with the then Soviet-Union. This friendship stood the ordeal of Chinese invasion of India in 1962. Thanks to this friendship India could emerge victorious in Bangladesh war of 1971 and turn the regional balance in favour of India. However, International politics witnessed unprecedented changes in the wake of globalisation and disintegration of Soviet Union as a composite state. But when a resurgent Russia emerged and the Indian economy was integrated with global economy, the friendship again revived and reached the height of privileged strategic partnership. Though USA tops the list of arms suppliers to India, of late, yet it supplies defensive weapons. But Russia has been a consistent arms suppliers to India and its supplies include offensive weapons also. A resurgent Russia is focusing attention on SEA. Russia's import from ASEAN has increased impressively which was 1.38% in 2001 and which touched 4.39% mark in 2016. The CAGR of Russia's import from ASEAN is higher than export to it. Singapore to the SEA nation is the one with whom Russia is found have the highest percentage of exports of total exports to ASEAN countries followed by Malaysia, Vietnam, Indonesia and Thailand. ASEAN is perceived as a rising center of power in Asia. A solid relationship could provide a greater balance in Russia's Asia policy, giving a boost to the multipolarity that ensures continuing Russian influence in world affairs in the face of American predominance. The ASEAN market holds much potential for Russia to exercise influence through its primary economic assets-arms and energy and for further diversification of economic relations. Putin's move is accordingly directed to attain the objective of diversifying away from arms and oil.

Not only that India and Russia in the globalised world, where geo-politics has taken the form of geo-economics, individually take interest in pursuing trade relations with SEA countries, but they jointly pursue trade interests in that area which prompted the present study i.e. Indo-Russian cooperation in SEA. Even in the political sphere they are found united in fight against terrorism which is the menacing cloud hovering over the political sky of the world in general and that of South Asia and SEA in particular. All the SEA countries are unanimous in their condemnation of terrorism. India and Russia carried on economic cooperation in SEA in the context of following items.

Defence Equipment

(i) Sukhoi 30

(ii) MiG

(iii) Brahmos

Oil

Roseneft-Essar

During the first decade of 21st century Vietnam and Indonesia purchased a significance proportion of their military hardware from Russia. Malayasia and Burma also started looking to Russia for modernising their forces. This process is continuing, HAL which is the symbol of Indo-Russian cooperation has International customers like Malayasia, Thailand, Vietnam. India is found acting as gateway or conduit for Russian trade with SEA in certain cases. Malaysia invited the deployment of an IAF training team to give training to their pilots on Su-30MKM aircraft. Similarly India trained the Vietnamese military in handling Russian built sub-marines like-wise the beginning of business in India by the oil company of Russia, Rosneft marked its expansion to SEA. Hence the observation is that India and Russia have collaborated in trade and other relations with certain SEA countries and India has acted as the gate way.

It can be mentioned that their cooperation has facilitated the process of unipolar moment of contemporary history giving way to a multipolar world. China has also contributed to the process. BRICS, RIC, SCO and other organisations have united these countries. It is true that Russia has come closer to China and India has come closer to USA. This is corroborated by some of the diplomat respondents also. But these relations do not impact Indo-Russian relations which have stood the test of time. In the globalised world each country can have cross-cutting relations without harming the core interests of the other. It will be not out of context to mention that India seeks to procure interceptor based S-400 from Russia overcoming US sanctions. Even Indonesia and Vietnam are hopeful of doing that.

To conclude finally, a multipolar world has benefitted India, Russia and even China. India and Russia in particular need to make efforts in the direction of retaining the democratic order. India wants a multipolar world and multipolar Asia. It needs to check terrorism along with Russia and South East Asian countries. It is interesting to note that the elite in Russia have a consensus regarding their cooperation with India. But this is lacking in case of their attitude towards China. Both India and Russia are genuinely interested not only in a multipolar world but also a multipolar Asia. But China is an elephant in the room as stressed by one diplomat respondent. It wants a multipolar world but a unipolar Asia. The SEA nations do not appreciate domination of any external power over them. Hence in the present changed scenario Indo-Russian cooperation is welcome in SEA nations. So a great responsibility lies on the shoulders of India and Russia in furthering the cause of a multipolar world and multipolar Asia.

References

- Abhinavharlalka, (2013)India and Russia- History and Beyond, policy pit, https://youthpolicydialogue.wordpress.com/2013, acessed on 15.04.2017
- Abhinavharlalka(2013) India and Russia- History and Beyond, Policy pit, https://youthpolicydialogue.wordpress.com/2013, February, 9, accessed on 15.04.2017
- Acharya, Mohanty (2012) Indo-Russian cooperation in SEA: A Move towards multipolar world, Anvesa, Vol. 7 (2)December.
- Acharya, Shyam Sundar (1992) 'India and the Super powers during Nehru era', The Orissa Political Science Journal, Vol. IX.
- Acharya, S.S, Mohanty, P.M (2012) Indo-Russia cooperation in SEA: A move towards Multipolar world, Anvesa, Vol.7(2), December, p.34.
- Acharya, Shyam Sundar (1990-91) 'India and the Super powers during Nehru era', The Orissa Political Science Journal, Vol. IX.
- Ambatkar, Sanjay (2002) 'India and ASEAN in the 21st Century', New Delhi, Anmol publications pvt. Ltd.
- Bagchi, Indrani, (2018) Times of India, India among top five friends of Moscow says Russian poll, 28, June.
- Bakshi, Jyotsna (2004) Russia China Relations: Relevance for India, Published by IDSA and Shipra, New Delhi.
- Bedi, Rahul (2003) Moscow looking east to counter U.S. Power, IPS News, www.ipsnews.net
- Blank, Stephen, (1999) Is There A Future For Russian Relations With Southeast Asia?, The Journal Of East Asian Affairs, Vol. 13, No. 1 (Spring/ Summer 1999), Pp. 73-110, Institute For National Security Strategy, http:/ /www.Jstor.Org/ Accessed on 02-11-2016
- Boquerat, Gilles & Grare, Frederic (2004) India, China, Russia intricacies of an Asian Triangle, India research press, New Delhi.
- Bulavinov, Ilya (2002) "Vladimir Putin Told the Indian Comrades Success of Russian Economy, " Kommersant, (Moscow), 5 December, p. 7.)
- Chenoy, Anuradha. M, (2010) India and Russia: Allies in the International Political System, P. Stobdan, India-Russia Strategic Partnership Common Perspectives, (eds.) IDSA, New Delhi, Pentagon Press, www.pentagonpress.in.p.p-165-177

- Chenoy, Anuradha. M.(2016) November, 5-11, India, Russia Forging ahead in changing times, Vol.XLI, No.32, Employment news weekly, New Delhi.
- Chenoy, Anuradha M. (2010) India and Russia: Allies in the International Political System, P. Stobdan, India-Russia Strategic Partnership Common Perspectives, (eds.) IDSA, New Delhi, Pentagon Press, www.pentagonpress.in.p.p-165-177
- Chenoy, Anuradha M. (2017) and Kumar, Rajan Re-emerging Russia: Structures, Institutions and Processes, Palgrave Macmillan.
- Das Kundu, Nivedita , (2017) India-Russia Relationship: Past, Present & Future. Valdai International Discussion Club, 2017, http./valdaiclub.com
- DasKundu, Nivedita (2016) India-Russia Relationship: Past, Present & Future, Valdai Discussion Club, http://valdaiclub.com accessed on 28.10.2017
- DasKundu, Nivedita (2006) Resurgence of Russian Economy, https://idsa.in/idsastrategiccomments.
- Dash, P. L. (2003) Putin's Visit in Perspective, Economic and Political Weekly, Vol. 38, No. 3 (Jan. 18-24, 2003), pp. 192-194.
- D'Agostino, Anthony April 13, (2017) How the Soviet Union Thought Itself to Death, http://nationalinterest.org, accessed on 15.04.2017
- De Souza, Lucio Vinhas, (2008) A Different Country: Russia's Economic Resurgence (Centre for European Policy Studies) Paperback – July 25, Centre for European Policy Studies.
- Dubey, Muchkund, (2012) 'Indo-(Soviet) Russian Relations', Mainstream Weekly, VOL L, No 40, September 22.
- Foot, Rosemary, et.al(ed.), (2003), US hegemony and International Organisations, the United States and Multilateral Institutions, Oxford University press, New york).
- Ganapathi, M.(2015) 'Look East - Act East' Dimension of India's Foreign Policy, Indian Foreign Affairs Journal Vol. 10, No. 1, January–March 2015, p.p.63-73
- Gill, Stephen, (1990) "American Hegemony and the trilateral commission", Cambridge University Press, New York.
- Gidadhubli, R. G.(1995) India's Exports to Russia: Complexities and Contradictions, Economic and Political Weekly, Vol. 30, No. 44, Nov.4 pp. 2780-2782, http://www.jstor.org/stable/4403389, Accessed on 02-11-2016
- Gohar, Bushra (1987) Indo-Soviet Relations: The Rajiv Era, Pakistan Horizon, Vol. 40, No. 3 (Third Quarter), pp. 94-124, Pakistan Institute of International Affairs, http://www.jstor.org/stable/41394736 Accessed on 02-11-2016
- Goh, Evelyn (2005) 'Great Powers and Southeast Asian Regional Security Strategies: Omni-Enmeshment, Balancing and Hierarchical Order', Institute of Defence and Strategic Studies.

- Harshe, Rajen (1998) India and Russia in a Changing World written, Economic and Political Weekly, Vol. 33, No. 9, Feb. 28 - Mar. 6, pp. 457-460, http://www.jstor.org/stable/4406461, Accessed on02-11-2016.
- Huntington, Samuel P. (1999)'The Lonely Superpower', Foreign affairs, March/April, www.foreignaffairs.com/articles, Accessed on 11.5.2016.
- Hughes, Lindsay (2016) The Indo-Russian Relationship: Old Imperatives, New Beginnings, strategic analysis paper, Future Directions International, http://www.futuredirections.org.au/, acessed on 15.04.2017
- Hughes, Lindsay (2016) The Indo-Russian Relationship: Old Imperatives, New Beginnings, strategic analysis paper, Future Directions International, http://www.futuredirections.org.au/, acessed on 15.04.2017
- Ijaz, Aymen, Russia's Resurgence: Global-Regional Threats and Opportunities, Journal of Current Affairs Vol. 1, Nos. 1&2: 30-50.
- Ilya Bulavinov, (2002) "Vladimir Putin Told the Indian Comrades Success of Russian Economy," Kommersant (Moscow), 5 December, p. 7.
- Jha, Pankaj Kumar (2011) India's Defence Diplomacy in Southeast Asia, Vol 5. No 1. January, Journal of Defence Studies.
- Jha, Pankaj Kumar (2011) 'India's Defence Diplomacy in South East Asia', Vol 5. No 1. January 2011, https://idsa.in/jds accessed on 19.2.2013
- Jinda, Arunrat (2017) Southeast Asia in Russian's Foreign Policy: New Player in the ASEAN countries, The macro-theme Review, 6(1), spring, A multidisciplinary journal of global macro trends.
- Jain, B.M., (2003) 'India and Russia: Reassessing the Time-Tested Ties', Pacific Affairs, University of British Columbia, Pacific Affairs, Vol. 76, No. 3, Fall, pp. 375-397, www.jstor.org, Accessed on 23-06-2016.
- Jain. B.M. (2003) India and Russia: Reassessing the Time-Tested Ties, Pacific Affairs, Vol. 76, No. 3, Fall, pp. 375-397, Pacific Affairs, University of British Columbia, www.jstor.org/stable/40023819, Accessed on 23-06-2016 09:01
- John, Cherian, (2000) "A Strategic Partnership, " Frontline, Vol. 17, No. 21 (14–27 October 2000, http://www.frontlineonnet.com/1721/17210100.htm.
- Kamalakaran, Ajay, (2014) Jawaharlal Nehru's Tryst with the USSR, Russia Beyond, www.rbth.com
- Kamboj, Anil, (2013) India's Foreign Policy in 21st century: Challenges Ahead, Vol. XXXIV, No.12, World focus, 408, December, p.p-9-17.
- Kapila, Subash (2000) India-Russia Strategic Cooperation: Time to Move Away, Paper No. 144, South Asia Analysis Group, http://www.southasiaanalysis.org.
- Kumar, Rajan (2001) Indo-Russian Relations and the Emerging International Power Structure', Journal of Peace Studies, Vol. 9.
- Mastny. Vojtech (2010) The Soviet Union's Partnership with India, Journal of Cold War Studies, Volume 12, Number 3, Summer, pp. 50-90, Published by The MIT Press.

- Mastny. Vojtech (2010) The Soviet Union's Partnership with India Journal of Cold War Studies, Vol. 12, No. 3, Summer, pp. 50-90.
- *Mansingh, Surjit (2016)* Indo-Soviet Relations in the Nehru years: the view from New Delhi, http://www.php.isn.ethz.ch, Accessed on 20.03.2017
- M Rasgotra & V D Chopra 'India's relations with Russia and China-A new Phase'
- Mohanty, Biswaranjan, (2012) Foreign policy of India in the 21st century, New century publication, New Delhi.
- Mohanty, Arun (2010) Evolution of Parliamentarism in Post soviet Russia, Axis publication, New Delhi.
- Mohanty, Arun (2010) Evolution of Parliamentarism in Post soviet Russia, Axis Publication, New Delhi.
- Mohanty, Arun (2010) 'Indo-Russian Trade and Economic Cooperation: The Way Ahead', P. Stobdan, India-Russia Strategic Partnership Common Perspectives, (eds.) IDSA, New Delhi, Pentagon Press, www.pentagonpress.in.p.p-165-177
- Murray, Donette (2013) Multipolarity in the 21st Century: A New World Order, Routledge publication.
- Palit, Amitendu (2016)India's Act East Policy and Implications for Southeast Asia, Southeast Asian Affairs, Volume 2016, ISEAS–Yusof Ishak Institute, pp. 81-91.
- Pande, Aparna and Thoburn, Hannah (2016)Why the India-Russia Relationship Works, What has kept this old friendship going, well into the early 21st century?, http://en.kremlin.ru/events/president/news
- Paramonov, Vladimir and Strokov, Aleksey Russian-Chinese relations: past, present and future' of Russian series on behalf of Conflict Studies Research Centre.
- Paradorn, Rangsimaporn, (2009), Russia's Search for Influence in Southeast Asia, Asian Survey, Vol. 49, No. 5, Published by University of California Press.
- Pattnaik, Ajaya, (2018) Putin - Modi Summit at Sochi: New Informality in India-Russia Relations, Mainstream, VOL LVI No 23 New Delhi May 26, 2018.
- Paau, Danny, Yee, Herbert (eds.)(2005), Return of the Dragon US-China Relations in the 21st Century, Peterlang GmbH
- Raghuramapatruni, Radha, (2012) India's Trade with the ASEAN: Realities and prospects, Abhijeet publication, New Delhi.
- Reddy, K. Raja (2012) 'Foreign Policy of India and Asia-Pacific' (ed.), New century publication, New Delhi.
- Rao, R. V. R, Chandrasekhara (1973) 'Indo-Soviet Economic Relations', Asian Survey, Vol. 13, No. 8, August, pp. 793-801, University of California Press, Stable URL: http://www.jstor.org/stable/2642868, Accessed on: 02-11-2016.

- *Surjit Mansingh (2016)* Indo-Soviet Relations in the Nehru years: the view from New Delhi, http://www.php.isn.ethz.ch, Accessed on 20.03.2017
- Stobdan, P. (2010) India-Russia Strategic Partnership Common Perspectives, (eds.) IDSA, New Delhi, Pentagon Press, www.pentagonpress.in
- Shaumyan. Tatiana. (2010) Russian-Indian Bilateral Cooperation, P. Stobdan, India-Russia Strategic Partnership Common Perspectives, (eds.) IDSA, New Delhi, Pentagon Press, www.pentagonpress.in.p.149-164.
- Singh, S.P. (1987) Political dimensions of India-USSR relations, Allied publishers pvt. Ltd.
- Sharma, Shri Ram, (1999) India-USSR Relations, 1947-1971: from Ambivalence to Steadfastness, Part 1, India - 1999 - 133 pages. Discovery Publishing House.
- Tan Tai Yong and See Chak Mun, (2009) The Evolution of India–ASEAN Relations, India Review, vol. 8, no. 1, January–March, pp. 20-42.
- Unnikrishnan, Nandan & Purushothaman, Uma in Observer Research Foundation.
- Yadav, Purva, (2012) India's changing trade pattern in the process of globalization, Procedia - Social and Behavioral Sciences 37, 157-166, www.sciencedirect.com
- Yadav, R.S. (2013) 'India as rising power: opportunities and challenges', Vol. XXXIV, No.12, World focus, 408, December, pp. 3-8.
- *Beuria, Abasara, 2018, Purva Bharata o' Indo-pacific, The samaj, 16th March*
- *Chakraborti, Tridib (2009)The distance proximity paradox: Unravelling India's ASEAN policy over three decades, India's Foreign Policy, A Ghosh, T Chakraborti & A.J Majumdar, S. Chatterjee (eds.), p. 267.*
- *Cabalza, Chester January 27, 2018, The Philippines' Strategic Relationship With India, The diplomat, https://thediplomat.com/2018/01/the-philippines-strategic-relationship-with-india.*
- *Ghosh, Abhijit(2009) India Russia: Towards New Strategic relations, 'India's Foreign Policy', (Eds.) Pearson Publication, New Delhi.*
- *Goswami, Namrata (2009) looking east through India's north east: identifying policy challenges and outlining the response, IDSA occasional paper No.2, New Delhi, June.*
- *Haokip, Thongkholal, 2010, Political Integration of Northeast India: A historical Analysis, strategic Analysis, Volume 36, issue 2, Routledge publication.*
- *Jha, Pankaj Kumar, 2011, India's defence diplomacy in South east Asia, Vol 5. No 1. January, Journal of Defence Studies.*
- *Mohanty, Biswaranjan, (2012) Foreign policy of India in the 21st century. New century publication, New Delhi.*
- *Mohanty, P M, Acharya, S.S, Panda, G. 2017, International Journal of Advance Research, Int. J. Adv. Res. 5(10), 1516-1529, www.journalijar.com*

- *Muni, S.D (2011) India's Look East Policy: The strategic dimension, ISAS Working paper, No. 121 – 1 February.*
- *Nanda, Prakash, (2003) Rediscovering Asia: Evolution of India's Look east Policy, Lancer publishers.*
- *Palit, Amitendu (2016) India's Act East Policy and Implications for Southeast Asia Southeast Asian Affairs, Volume, pp. 81-91 (Article) Published by ISEAS–Yusof Ishak Institute, Project Muse.*
- *Roy Chaudhury, Dipanjan, India's Act East policy complements Asean's Act West strategy January 24, 2018, Economic Times, economictimes.indiatimes.com.*
- *Sajjanhar, Ashok (2016) 2 Years On, Has Modi's 'Act East' Policy Made a Difference for India?, The Diplomat, http://thediplomat.com.*
- *Singh, Vishal(1978)India and South East Asia, International studies,, Quarterly journal of JNU, Vol.17, number3-4, Vikash Publishing Home Pvt. Ltd, New Press.*
- *Singh, Yogendra, North east in india's look east policy, report of the IPCS seminar 2008.*
- Tharoor, Shasi, 2012, Pax Indica India and the world of the 21st century.
- *Yadav, R.S. 2011, Changing contours of India's Neighbourhood policy, World focus, Indo-centric foreign affairs, monthly journal, Vol. XXXII, No. 6, G.Kishore Babu, Delhi.*
- *ASEAN rising — on India-Southeast Asia cooperation, The Hindu, Editorial, JANUARY 26, 2018, www.thehindu.com*
- *Discovery of Asia: India and Asean should join to establish the world's most dynamic economic zone, January 24, 2018, 2:00 AM IST TOI Edit in TOI Editorial)*
- *Northeast Region Vision 2020*
- Greenstein, Fred I.(1972) "Personality and Politics', Problem of evidence, inference and conceptualization in S.M Lipset (ed.) Politics and Social Sciences, NewDelhi, pp. 163-206.
- July 20th, 2015 by Anubhav Gupta, India and APEC: Charting a Path to Membership, ASPI Issue Brief, Asia Society policy institute, asiasociety.org
- Gnanasagaran, Angaindrankumar, 19 February 2018, Arms trade fuels Russia's inroads into Southeast Asia, The ASEAN post, /theaseanpost.com
- Guilford, J.P(1959)Personality, New York, pp. 5-6.
- Jinda, Arunrat (2017) Southeast Asia in Russian's Foreign Policy: New Player in the ASEAN countries, The macro-theme Review, 6(1), spring 2017, A multidisciplinary journal of global macro trends.
- Jinda, Arunrat, The Macro theme Review 6(1), Spring 2017, Southeast Asia in Russian's Foreign Policy: New Player in the ASEAN countries.
- Klyuchanskaya S. Nuclear Energy in Southeast Asia and Russia's Interests; A Russian Journal on International Security, vol. 4, 2011, pp. 66-78.

- Putra, Nur Azha & Andrews-Speed, Philip (2018) Prospects for Nuclear Power in ASEAN, The diplomat.
- Samuel Ramani, June 24, 2016, Cambodia: Russia's Gateway to ASEAN? Russia's outreach to Cambodia is part of a larger strategy to increase influence in Southeast Asia. The Diplomat, accessed on 17/1/2018.
- Sharma, Ruchira(2018)The many faces of Putin, Times of India, 22 March
- Sharma, Ruchira(2018)The many faces of Putin, Times of India, 22 March
- Sharma, Ruchira(2018)The many faces of Putin, Times of India, 22 March
- Sumsky, Victor. (2011). East Asian summit and Russia: Long-awaited invitation. Security Index: A Russian Journal on International Security, 17(2), 63–68.
- Thambipillai, Pushpa Southeast Asia, Russia and the Ex-Soviet Republics: Expanding the Links, Contemporary Southeast Asia, Vol. 16, No. 1 (June 1994), p. 102)
- Thambipillai, Pushpa, Southeast Asia, Russia and the Ex-Soviet Republics: Expanding the Links, Contemporary Southeast Asia, Vol. 16, No. 1 (June 1994), pp. 93-107)
- Tsvetov, Anton ASEAN and Russia Look to Achieve Their Full Potential, RIAC, May 20, 2016.
- Tsvetov, Anton, Russia And ASEAN: In Search Of Economic Synergy And Political Consensus, Russian International Affairs Council, http://Russiancouncil.Ru/En/Analytics, June, 2016.
- Tsvetov, Anton, Russia Still Seeking a Role in ASEAN, 19.05.2016, carnegie Moscow center, http.carnegie.ru
- Tsvetov, Anton (2016) Russia And Asean: In Search Of Economic Synergy And Political Consensus, Russian International Affairs Council, Http://Russiancouncil.Ru/En/Analytics, June, 2016.
- Yaroslav, Lissovolik, . (2012). Russia looks east: Modernization plans and cooperation with ASEAN. In Victor Sumsky, Mark Hong, & Amy Lugg (Eds.), ASEAN-Russia: Foundations and future prospects (pp. 245–253). Singapore: ISEAS.
- TOI, Editorial, May, 9, 2018, p.12 Vlad the strongman
- ASEAN Today, 2018, March 14, Putin uses arms sales to ASEAN to increase Russian standing in Southeast Asia, /www.aseantoday.com
- ASEAN Today, 2018, May 10, Strengthened ASEAN-Russian military links are a signal Russia is serious about its pivot to Asia, /www.aseantoday.com
- Acharya, Shyam Sundar, India and the super powers during Nehru Era, The Orissa Political Science Journal, Vol. IX, 1992.
- Acharya, Shyam Sundar, 2014, Joint Indo-US Counter terrorism measures: Areflection of transformation in their mutual relations, An interdisciplinary Research Journal, Vol. 9, issue-1.
- Baruah, Sanjib Kr India, Russia To Take Part In Massive Tri-Service Drill, The Asian Age., www.asianage.com Accessed On 4.1.2018

- Chanda, Nayan, Wooing by weapons, Times of India, 28 July, 2018, p. 10.
- Chellaney, Brahma, US extraterritorial sanctions: Begging for a waiver now is the worst possible option for India, Times of India, May 31, 2018, p. 12.
- Chellaney, Brahma, US extraterritorial sanctions: Begging for a waiver now is the worst possible option for India, Times of India, May 31, 2018, p. 12.
- Chenoy, Anuradha M. India, Russia And The Shift In Global Balance Of Power Does Russia Matter In India's Foreign Policy? Indian Foreign Affairs Journal Vol. 5, No. 3, July–September 2010, 263-289)
- Choudhary, Sanjeev Feb 08, 2018, State refiners, RIL and Rosneft plan expansion, http.//economictimes.indiatimes.com/.
- Connolly, Richard and Sendstad, Cecilie, (2017) Russia's Role as an Arms Exporter, Russia and Eurasia Programme | March, Research Paper, The Strategic and Economic Importance of Arms Exports for Russia.
- Dutta, Sanjay, India balances US energy ties with $25bn Russian Gas deal, Times of IndiaJune 5, 2018.
- Franz-Stefan Gady, June 23, 2017, India, Russia Sign 'Military Cooperation Roadmap', The diplomats.
- John, Nevin, (2017) How Essar-Rosneft deal will change India's oil map?, New Delhi Last Updated: August 22, Business Today.
- Kumar, Amit, 'The Indian Navy Chief 's Visit and Indo-Russian Defence Cooperation', *IDSA Comment*, 29 July 2011, available at http://www. idsa.in, accessed on 29 June 2012.
- Rajeswari Pillai Rajagopalan, March 02, 2018, Why the Vietnam President's India Visit Matters for Security Ties, 2018 The Diplomat.
- Tharoor, Shasi, 2012, Pax Indica India and the world of the 21st century, p. 189.
- Tsvetov, Anton, Russia still seeking a role in ASEAN, carnegie.ru/ commentary, 19.5.2016.
- Tsvetov, Anton April 21, 2016, Did Russia Just Side With China on the South China Sea?, The diplomat, thediplomat.com)
- Zakharov, Aleksei, 2017, Exploring New Drivers In India-Russia Cooperation, Occasional Papers Oct 12, Https://Www.Orfonline.Org/ Research/Exploring-New-Drivers-India-Russia-Cooperation
- Business standard, New Delhi, 26th January 2018.
- Business standard, New Delhi, 25th January 2018.
- The Indian Express, Russia continues to be India's largest defence partner| Published: February 22, 2017, New Delhi, http./indianexpress.com
- Times of India, 2018, May 15, Bhubaneswar, p. 7.
- Pandit, Rajat (2022) India to deploy 2nd S-400 squadron at China front as PLA jets buzz near LAC, Times of India, July, 25.
- The Indian Express, Russia continues to be India's largest defence partner, Published: February 22, 2017, New Delhi, http./indianexpress.com.

- *Tharoor, Shasi, Pax Indica, India & the world of the 21st century, Penguin Groups, New Delhi, 2012 p. 425.*
- *Nathan A. Sears, China, Russia, and the Long 'Unipolar Moment', April 27, 2016, The diplomats.*
- *Anuradha M. Chenoy, India, Russia And The Shift In Global Balance Of Power Does Russia Matter In India's Foreign Policy?, Indian Foreign Affairs Journal Vol. 5, No. 3, July–September 2010, 263-289.*
- Chenoy, Anuradha M., 'India and Russia: Allies in the International Political System', in P. Stobdan (ed.), *India-Russia Strategic Partnership: Common, Perspectives*, New Delhi: Institute for Defence Studies and Analyses, 2010, pp. 131-48.
- Weitz, Richard, 'Is BRICS a Real Bloc?', *The Diplomat*, 22 April 2011, available at http://the-diplomat.com/2011/04/22/is-brics-a-real-bloc, accessed on 29 June 2012.
- Weitz, Richard, (2012) The Maturing of Russia-India Defence Relations, *Journal of Defence Studies, Vol. 6, No. 3, July, Institute for Defence Studies and Analyses, pp. 75-98.*
- *Kortunov, Andrey, Why the world is not becoming multipolar, RIAC, 27 June, 2018.*
- *Denny Roy "China's Pitch s Pitch for a Multipolar for a Multipolar World: The New Security Concept The New Security", Asia-Pacific Security AsiaPacific Security Studies. Accessed on 17 June, 2016.http://apcss.org/Publications/APSSS/ChinasPitchforaMultipolarWo rld.pdf*
- *Mohanty, Arun 2017, Indo-Russian relations under UPA rule, EURASIAN STATES socio-economic and political processes, Arun Mohanty, Ajay Pattnaik (eds.)KW publishers Pvt. Ltd.*
- *Kulkarni, Sneha, India-Russia relations as a key variables for global centers of power, World focus, July, 2018.*
- *(Nandan Unnikrishnan, Uma Purushothaman, 2015, Trends In Russia-China Relations Implications For India, Observer Research Foundation, Vinset Advertising, Delhi.)*
- *TOI, May, 9, 2018, p. 12 Vlad the strongman)*
- *Andrey Sushentsov, The India-China Rivalry And Russia's Interests, Valdai discussion club, 9.2.2018 http://valdaiclub.com, acessed on 10th April 2018.*
- *Patnaik, Ajay (2018) Putin - Modi Summit at Sochi: New Informality in India-Russia Relations, Mainstream, VOL LVI No 23 New Delhi May 26.*
- *'China and Russia are quasi allies ... On strategic affairs Russia and India have serious conversations only at top level', February 28, 2018, 2:03 AM IST Indrani Bagchiin Globes potting | Edit Page, India, Q&A, World | TOI)*
- *(Goa Declaration at 8th BRICS Summit, October 16, 2016, www.mea.gov.in)*
- *Abanti Bhattacharya, The Fallacy in the Russia-India-China Triangle, Strategic Analysis, Vol. 28, No. 2, Apr-Jun 2004, Institute for Defence Studies and Analyses)*

- *(Z. Mian et al., "Fissile Materials in South Asia and the Implications of the U.S.-India Nuclear Deal, "Science and Global Security 14, No, 2-3, 117 (2006).)*
- *Thapliyal, Maj Gen Sheru(2010) Implications of China's rise, Indian Defence Review, 26-3 July-Sep. 2010)*
- *Tharoor, Shasi, Pax Indica, India & the world of the 21st century, Penguin Groups, New Delhi, 2012.*
- *.(Mansingh, S. Rising China and Emergent India in the Twenty First Century, in Bajpai, K. and Pant, Harsh(ed.) India's Foreign Policy A reader, Oxford University Press, New Delhi, 2013 p. 296)*
- *Tharoor, Shasi, Pax Indica, India & the world of the 21st century, Penguin Groups, New Delhi, 2012, p. 186.*
- *Tharoor, Shasi, Pax Indica, India & the world of the 21st century, Penguin Groups, New Delhi, 2012 pp. 192-193)*

Index

C

D

E

F

G

N

O

S